Junípero Serra

Consulting Editors

Rodolfo Cardona
professor of Spanish
and comparative literature,
Boston University

James Cockcroft
visiting professor of Latin American
and Caribbean studies,
State University of New York at Albany

Hispanics of Achievement

Junípero Serra

Sean Dolan

Chelsea House Publishers
New York   Philadelphia

CHELSEA HOUSE PUBLISHERS

Editor-in-Chief: Remmel Nunn
Managing Editor: Karyn Gullen Browne
Copy Chief: Juliann Barbato
Picture Editor: Adrian G. Allen
Art Director: Maria Epes
Deputy Copy Chief: Mark Rifkin
Assistant Art Director: Noreen Romano
Manufacturing Manager: Gerald Levine
Systems Manager: Lindsey Ottman
Production Manager: Joseph Romano
Production Coordinator: Marie Claire Cebrián

Hispanics of Achievement
Senior Editor: John W. Selfridge

Staff for JUNÍPERO SERRA
Associate Editor: Philip Koslow
Copy Editor: Joseph Roman
Editorial Assistant: Martin Mooney
Picture Researcher: Vicky Haluska
Cover Illustration: John Paul Genzo

3 5 7 9 8 6 4 2

Library of Congress Cataloging-in-Publication Data
Dolan, Sean.
   Junípero Serra/Sean Dolan.
      p. cm.—(Hispanics of achievement)
   Includes bibliographical references and index.
   Summary: Focuses on the achievements of the 18-century Spanish
missionary who was one of the early explorers of California.
   ISBN 0-7910-1255-7
        0-7910-1282-4 (pbk.)
   1. Serra, Junípero 1713–84—Juvenile literature. 2. Explorers—
California—Biography—Juvenile literature. 3. Explorers—Spain—
Biography—Juvenile literature. 4. Franciscans—California—
Biography— Juvenile literature. 5. Franciscans—Missions— Califor-
nia—History—18th century—Juvenile literature. 6. Indians of North
America—California—Missions— Juvenile literature. 7. California—
History—To 1846—Juvenile literature. [1. Serra, Junípero, 1713–84.
2. Explorers. 3. Missionaries. 4. California—History—To 1846.]
I. Title II. Series.
F864.S44D65 1991   91-6863
979.4'02'092—dc20   CIP
[B]   AC

Contents

Hispanics of Achievement

Joan Baez
Mexican-American folksinger

Rubén Blades
Panamanian lawyer and entertainer

Jorge Luis Borges
Argentine writer

Juan Carlos
King of Spain

Pablo Casals
Spanish cellist and conductor

Miguel de Cervantes
Spanish writer

Cesar Chavez
Mexican-American labor leader

El Cid
Spanish military leader

Roberto Clemente
Puerto Rican baseball player

Salvador Dalí
Spanish painter

Plácido Domingo
Spanish singer

Gloria Estefan
Cuban-American singer

Gabriel García Márquez
Colombian writer

Pancho Gonzales
Mexican-American tennis player

Francisco José de Goya
Spanish painter

Frida Kahlo
Mexican painter

José Martí
Cuban revolutionary and poet

Rita Moreno
Puerto Rican singer and actress

Pablo Neruda
Chilean poet and diplomat

Antonia Novello
U.S. surgeon general

Octavio Paz
Mexican poet and critic

Pablo Picasso
Spanish artist

Anthony Quinn
Mexican-American actor

Oscar de la Renta
Dominican fashion designer

Diego Rivera
Mexican painter

Linda Ronstadt
Mexican-American singer

Antonio López de Santa Anna
Mexican general and politician

George Santayana
Spanish philosopher and poet

Andrés Segovia
Spanish guitarist

Junípero Serra
Spanish missionary and explorer

Lee Trevino
Mexican-American golfer

Diego Velázquez
Spanish painter

Pancho Villa
Mexican revolutionary

CHELSEA HOUSE PUBLISHERS

INTRODUCTION

Hispanics of Achievement

Rodolfo Cardona

The Spanish language and many other elements of Spanish culture are present in the United States today and have been since the country's earliest beginnings. Some of these elements have come directly from the Iberian Peninsula; others have come indirectly, by way of Mexico, the Caribbean basin, and the countries of Central and South America.

Spanish culture has influenced America in many subtle ways, and consequently many Americans remain relatively unaware of the extent of its impact. The vast majority of them recognize the influence of Spanish culture in America, but they often do not realize the great importance and long history of that influence. This is partly because Americans have tended to judge the Hispanic influence in the United States in statistical terms rather than to look closely at the ways in which individual Hispanics have profoundly affected American culture. For this reason, it is fitting that Americans obtain more than a passing acquaintance with the origins of these Spanish cultural elements and gain an understanding of how they have been woven into the fabric of American society.

It is well documented that Spanish seafarers were the first to explore and colonize many of the early territories of what is today called the United States of America. For this reason, students of geography discover Hispanic names all over the map of the United States. For instance, the Strait of Juan de Fuca was named after the Spanish explorer who first navigated the waters of the Pacific Northwest; the names of states such as Arizona (arid zone), Montana (mountain), Florida (thus named because it was reached on Easter Sunday, which in Spanish is called the feast of Pascua Florida), and California (named after a fictitious land in one of the first and probably the most popular among the Spanish novels of chivalry, *Amadis of Gaul*) are all derived from Spanish; and there are numerous mountains, rivers, canyons, towns, and cities with Spanish names throughout the United States.

Not only explorers but many other illustrious figures in Spanish history have helped define American culture. For example, the 13th-century king of Spain, Alfonso X, also known as the Learned, may be unknown to the majority of Americans, but his work on the codification of Spanish law has greatly influencedthe evolution of American law, particularly in the jurisdictions of the Southwest. For this contribution a statue of him stands in the rotunda of the Capitol in Washington, D.C. Likewise, the name Diego Rivera may be unfamiliar to most Americans, but this Mexican painter influenced many American artists whose paintings, commissioned during the Great Depression and the New Deal era of the 1930s, adorn the walls of government buildings throughout the United States. In recent years the contributions of Puerto Ricans, Mexicans, Mexican Americans (Chicanos), and Cubans in American cities such as Boston, Chicago, Los Angeles, Miami, Minneapolis, New York, and San Antonio have been enormous.

The importance of the Spanish language in this vast cultural complex cannot be overstated. Spanish, after all, is second only to English as the most widely spoken of Western languages within the United States as well as in the entire world. The popularity of the Spanish language in America has a long history.

In addition to Spanish exploration of the New World, the great Spanish literary tradition served as a vehicle for bringing the language and culture to America. Interest in Spanish literature in America began when English immigrants brought with them translations of Spanish masterpieces of the Golden Age. As early as 1683, private libraries in Philadelphia and Boston contained copies of the first picaresque novel, *Lazarillo de Tormes*, translations of Francisco de Quevedo's *Los Sueños*, and copies of the immortal epic of reality and illusion *Don Quixote*, by the great Spanish writer Miguel de Cervantes. It would not be surprising if Cotton Mather, the arch-Puritan, read *Don Quixote* in its original Spanish, if only to enrich his vocabulary in preparation for his writing *La fe del cristiano en 24 artículos de la Institución de Cristo, enviada a los españoles para que abran sus ojos* (The Christian's Faith in 24 Articles of the Institution of Christ, Sent to the Spaniards to Open Their Eyes), published in Boston in 1699.

Over the years, Spanish authors and their works have had a vast influence on American literature—from Washington Irving, John Steinbeck, and Ernest Hemingway in the novel to Henry Wadsworth Longfellow and Archibald MacLeish in poetry. Such important American writers as James Fenimore Cooper, Edgar Allan Poe, Walt Whitman, Mark Twain, and Herman Melville all owe a sizable debt to the Spanish literary tradition. Some writers, such as Willa Cather and Maxwell Anderson, who explored Spanish themes they came into contact with in the American Southwest and Mexico, were influenced less directly but no less profoundly.

Important contributions to a knowledge of Spanish culture in the United States were also made by many lesser known individuals—teachers, publishers, historians, entrepreneurs, and others—with a love for Spanish culture. One of the most significant of these contributions was made by Abiel Smith, a Harvard College graduate of the class of 1764, when he bequeathed stock worth $20,000 to Harvard for the support of a professor of French and Spanish. By 1819 this endowment had produced enough income to appoint a professor, and the philologist and humanist George Ticknor became the first holder of the Abiel Smith Chair, which was the very first endowed Chair at Harvard University. Other illustrious holders of the Smith Chair would include the poets Henry Wadsworth Longfellow and James Russell Lowell.

A highly respected teacher and scholar, Ticknor was also a collector of Spanish books, and as such he made a very special contribution to America's knowledge of Spanish culture. He was instrumental in amassing for Harvard libraries one of the first and most impressive collections of Spanish books in the United States. He also had a valuable personal collection of Spanish books and manuscripts, which he bequeathed to the Boston Public Library.

With the creation of the Abiel Smith Chair, Spanish language and literature courses became part of the curriculum at Harvard, which also went on to become the first American university to offer graduate studies in Romance languages. Other colleges and universities throughout the United States gradually followed Harvard's example, and today Spanish language and culture may be studied at most American institutions of higher learning.

No discussion of the Spanish influence in the United States, however brief, would be complete without a mention of the Spanish influence on art. Important American artists such as John Singer Sargent, James A. M. Whistler, Thomas Eakins, and Mary Cassatt all explored Spanish subjects and experimented with Spanish techniques. Virtually every serious American artist living today has studied the work of the Spanish masters as well as the great 20th-century Spanish painters Salvador Dalí, Joan Miró, and Pablo Picasso.

The most pervasive Spanish influence in America, however, has probably been in music. Compositions such as Leonard Bernstein's *West Side Story*, the Latinization of William Shakespeare's *Romeo and Juliet* set in New York's Puerto Rican quarter, and Aaron Copland's *Salon Mexico* are two obvious examples. In general, one can hear the influence of Latin rhythms—from tango to mambo, from guaracha to salsa—in virtually every form of American music.

This series of biographies, which Chelsea House has published under the general title HISPANICS OF ACHIEVEMENT, constitutes further recognition of—and a renewed effort to bring forth to the consciousness of America's young people—the contributions that Hispanic people have made not only in the United States but throughout the civilized world. The men and women who are featured in this series have attained a high level of accomplishment in their respective fields of endeavor and have made a permanent mark on American society.

The title of this series must be understood in its broadest possible sense: The term *Hispanics* is intended to include Spaniards, Spanish Americans, and individuals from many countries whose language and culture have either direct or indirect Spanish origins. The names of many of the people included in this series will be immediately familiar; others will be less recognizable. All, however, have attained recognition within their own countries, and often their fame has transcended their borders.

The series HISPANICS OF ACHIEVEMENT thus addresses the attainments and struggles of Hispanic people in the United States and seeks to tell the stories of individuals whose personal and professional lives in some way reflect the larger Hispanic experience. These stories are exemplary of what human beings can accomplish, often against daunting odds and by extraordinary personal sacrifice, where there is conviction and determination. Fray Junípero Serra, the 18th-century Spanish Franciscan missionary, is one such individual. Although in very poor health, he devoted the last 15 years of his life to the foundation of missions throughout California—then a mostly unsettled expanse of land—in an effort to bring a better life to Native Americans through the cultivation of crafts and animal husbandry. An example from recent times, the Mexican-American labor leader Cesar Chavez has battled bitter opposition and made untold personal sacrifices in his effort to help poor agricultural workers who have been exploited for decades on farms throughout the Southwest.

The talent with which each one of these men and women may have been endowed required dedication and hard work to develop and become fully realized. Many of them have enjoyed rewards for their efforts during their own lifetime, whereas others have died poor and unrecognized. For some it took a long time to achieve their goals, for others success came at an early age, and for still others the struggle continues. All of them, however, stand out as people whose lives have made a difference, whose achievements we need to recognize today and should continue to honor in the future.

Junípero Serra

Father Junípero Serra, portrayed in the coarse gray robes that he wore after joining the Franciscan order in 1731, at the age of 18. Serra earned renown as a philosopher and preacher on his native island of Majorca, but in 1749 he left everything behind and went to the New World as a missionary.

CHAPTER ONE

A Crisis of Faith

Father Junípero Serra was troubled. Even among his fellow Franciscans, who had taken vows of chastity, poverty, and obedience in order to do what they saw as God's work, Father Serra was renowned for his devotion. (The Franciscans were members of the Roman Catholic religious order founded in 1209 by St. Francis of Assisi and dedicated to the ideal of imitating the life of Christ, especially his poverty.) Father Serra was accustomed to performing his daily duties with a cheerful zeal, but lately his colleagues had noticed that the diminutive padre—Serra was no more than five feet, two inches tall—whose faith and learning were greater than all of theirs, did not smile as often as usual. He seemed preoccupied and distracted, except when reciting the prayers of his Divine Office or when singing the hymns that he loved so much. (The Divine Office is the series of prayers offered by a Roman Catholic priest at the seven canonical hours into which the day is divided. Customarily, matins and lauds are offered at midnight, prime and terce at 6:00 A.M., sext and none at 11:00 A.M., vespers and compline at 7:00 P.M.) At those times, his prayers took on a new fervency, as if he were hoping that by a greater demonstration of his faith he would receive some answer to whatever was disturbing him.

It was the first crisis of faith that the 35-year-old priest had suffered. Looking back, he was unable to remember a time when he had not wanted to be a priest. He recalled the day in 1728 when as a boy of 15 he made the 25-mile journey with his parents—he and his father on foot, his mother on the back of a donkey—from their home village of Petra on the island of Majorca to the capital city of Palma. In Palma, his parents brought him to the great cathedral and delivered him into the hands of a priest for religious and intellectual training. How sad he had been that day, as his quiet, dignified parents took their leave of him, and how glad when he realized that he was at last getting on with the real business of his life. He also remembered the day three years later—September 15, 1731, the happiest day of his life—when he at last professed his vows as a member of the Order of St. Francis. Truly, he felt, his life had begun on that day, when he donned for good the Franciscan monk's rough-hewn gray robe and cowl, with its belt of white rope knotted three times, and the modest sandals worn by the members of the order. Each year, he devoutly celebrated that date with a mass, and he never ceased to believe, as he often stated, that "all good things came to me with this profession." The day, six years later, when he was ordained as a priest was no less sacred to him.

He had achieved much since his ordination. Along with his capacity for faith and his cheerful good nature, Serra had been blessed with a keen intellect, one equally capable of grappling with practical questions as with the knottiest problems of philosophy and theology. Even before becoming a priest, he had achieved a professorship at the Convent of San Francisco (Spanish for St. Francis), whose priests were as famous for their scholarship as for their religious zeal. He received a doctorate in sacred theology and attained many honors for both his scholarship and his preaching.

The cloister at the Convent of San Francisco in Palma, Majorca, where Serra studied to become a priest. He so distinguished himself in philosophy and theology that he was appointed to a professorship at the convent at the age of 23.

The most important addresses and sermons of the year were often reserved for Father Junípero Serra. He was both respected and loved, and he believed that he was doing important work, God's work. He never, not even for an instant, doubted the rightness of the course his life had taken.

But for the first time, in the last months of 1748, Father Serra had reason to doubt himself, and it was this that had brought about his crisis. Word had reached the Convent of San Francisco that a special representative of the church had just arrived in Spain. This man, Father Pedro Pérez de Mezquía, was the special representative of the Apostolic College of San Fernando in Mexico City, the seat of the government of Spain's colonies in the New World. The Apostolic College of San Fernando was one of four institutions in Mexico that had been established for the purpose of training missionaries to convert the Indians of the New World to Catholicism. Father Mezquía had come to Spain for the purpose of recruiting prospective missionaries for the Apostolic College. Such special representatives made the long, arduous, and dangerous voyage to Spain from Mexico only once every 10 or 15 years.

Father Mezquía had been sent because both the church and the king were in desperate need of devoted priests to serve as missionaries to the Pame Indians of the rugged Sierra Gorda region of Mexico. Until recently, the Pame had been steadfast in their resistance to the representatives of Spanish civilization. They had clung to their traditional way of life, refusing the entreaties of Spanish priests to live as agricultural laborers on mission lands. On occasion, they had attacked and burned the Spanish settlements, terrorizing soldier and civilian alike. Recently, some inroads had been made by missionaries; but diseases transmitted by the Spanish had devastated the Pame population, and even the cooperative Indians had abandoned the missions for their mountain strongholds.

It was Mezquía's mission that precipitated Serra's crisis of conscience. Even before becoming a Franciscan, during the probationary period known as the novitiate, Serra had dreamed of becoming a missionary, which he considered a priest's highest calling. The Franciscans had a great tradition as missionaries; gray-robed Franciscans had preached to the unconverted in Palestine, North Africa, Persia, India, and eastern Russia as well as in Europe and the New World. Serra had read and been taken with the histories of the order and the chronicles of its celebrated missionaries, particularly St. Francis Solano, the priest who according to church tradition single-handedly converted thousands of South American Indians while roaming Peru playing his violin. The Apostolic College's need for missionaries coincided with Serra's long-held desire to "serve God better and to save my soul." But to his dismay, he hesitated to answer Mezquía's appeal.

For the first time, Serra found himself asking if perhaps God was expecting too much from him. No one could question his zeal and commitment to the Lord's service. He examined his conscience and found that he had given all of himself to his vocation, faithfully, joyously, and selflessly. Aside from his Bible and prayer book, he had only two earthly possessions—a bed made of rough wooden planks, on which he slept without a mattress, and a large crucifix, almost two feet in length, which he clasped to his breast while sleeping. He ate sparingly and allowed himself only the simplest of pleasures, the occasional company and conversation of friends.

Now, it seemed, he was asked to make an even greater sacrifice, to leave behind the only home he had known, the beautiful Mediterranean island of Majorca, with its rolling hills and olive

St. Francis Solano (1549–1610), a Franciscan missionary, was credited with baptizing hundreds of thousands of Indians throughout the Spanish dominions in South America. Solano's example inspired Junípero Serra to leave his home for the perilous life of a missionary.

groves, its farms and fishing villages, its stone walls, its lookout towers constructed on the coast to guard against pirates, its magnificent spires and churches. He would have to leave these beloved surroundings as well as his family and friends for the parched mountains and deserts of Mexico. He would also have to leave behind his respected position, in which he had done so much good work, for the hazardous life of a missionary among the savage, heathen Indians of the New World.

There was nothing compelling him to do this, of course, except his own highly developed sense of conscience and duty. Father Mezquía had not sailed the Atlantic just to pluck him, Junípero Serra, out of Majorca to serve in the Apostolic College of San Fernando. Mezquía was in Spain; he would no doubt find there plenty of volunteers for the missions. No one would think badly of Serra if he did not speak up. None of the other priests at San Francisco, all of them good and devout men, was volunteering. Yet it gnawed at Father Serra each day that he was hanging back, even as he reflected on how much he would hate to leave his home island. To become a missionary in the New World would mean in all likelihood to say good-bye forever to his mother and father, his younger sister, brother-in-law, and nephew, for very few missionaries ever returned. Sickness ran rampant in the New World, and more than a few missionaries there had died the sanctified death of the martyr at the hands of those they had been sent to save.

So each day the tiny priest prayed. At times, like Jesus in the garden at Gethsemane, he cried, "Let this cup pass from me"; at other times, he appealed for the strength to carry out what he believed in his heart to be his rightful duty. Tormented, he walked the cloistered gardens of the grounds of San Francisco and visited the church's 23 chapels, where he asked guidance from the various saints and martyrs. Sometimes, when he reflected that Jesus had not used his miraculous powers to escape his crucifixion on the cross, he grew exultant and longed to embrace his destiny. At other moments, when he remembered the jeering mob that mocked

Christ and the nails that tore his flesh, he grew fearful and prayed that he be allowed to escape this fate, which he felt was being pushed inexorably upon him. Always, he asked that his anguished soul be put at rest.

At last, Father Serra reached a decision. In confidence, he told the father superior of the convent that he wished to volunteer as a member of Father Mezquía's mission. Word was sent to Father Mezquía in Spain. To his surprise and delight, Serra learned that another member of the convent, his former pupil and beloved friend Francisco Palóu, had been privately wrestling with the same decision and had finally determined to volunteer as a missionary. The knowledge that such a kindred spirit would accompany him to Mexico helped ease Father Serra's lingering doubts. He felt as though he had received a sign from God.

The reply came from Spain. It seemed that the volunteers from the Convent of San Francisco had sent word too late, for Mezquía had already filled his complement of 33 missionaries. The cup had passed, and Serra had not been made to drink from it. But in February 1749, a second message arrived, this one from the port at Cádiz, in southern Spain, where the 33 priests had assembled to embark for the New World. On beholding the rough waves of the wintry Atlantic, five priests had reconsidered their decision to become missionaries. Did Fathers Serra and Palóu wish to take their place?

The interior of the Cathedral of Palma in Majorca. At the age of 15, Miguel Serra was brought to the cathedral by his parents and turned over to a priest for religious instruction. After deciding that his destiny was to be a missionary, Serra never returned to his parents' house.

CHAPTER TWO

From Majorca to Mexico

The island of Majorca, located in the Mediterranean Sea 100 miles off the eastern coast of Spain, is an Edenic place. The largest of the Balearic Islands, it is blessed with a pleasurable climate, ample rainfall, and gentle, cooling breezes. Although Majorca is comparatively small (approximately 1,405 square miles in area) its landscape contains a wealth of diversity. Two mountain ranges traverse opposite sides of the isle from southwest to northeast; geologically, these are continuations of the great sierras of Andalusia on the Iberian mainland. The western range, whose highest peak is the Puig Mayor, is the taller and more rugged, with an average elevation of more than 4,000 feet and sheer, rocky cliffs. The eastern range is more properly a tall plateau, with an average elevation of 1,000 feet, and is famous for its stalactite caves, among the most spectacular in Europe. Hidden deep within some of these underground caverns are inky, bottomless lakes.

From these mountains, in any direction, one gazes upon the shimmering waters of the Mediterranean. Majorcan life is dominated by the sea. For hundreds of years, the coasts have been lined with small fishing villages whose inhabitants, in wooden dories, venture onto the water to harvest tuna and lobster and to sell their catch and the island's many agricultural products at villages and ports in Spain and France. Over the centuries, the sea has also brought to Majorca's shores a host of would-be raiders and conquerors, drawn by the island's agricultural riches and pleasing vistas. The Mediterranean's first great seafaring people, the Phoenicians, came to Majorca as early as the 10th century B.C. and were followed by the ancient Egyptians, Greeks, and Romans. It is said that Hannibal, the brilliant general from Carthage who crossed the Alps in an attempt to conquer Rome, recruited his talented stone throwers from Majorca. The Moors, North African adherents of the religion of Islam, occupied Majorca in A.D. 797 as part of their attempt to subjugate the Iberian Peninsula. The Turks, the Moors' successors as the dominant force of Islam, also attempted to conquer the Majorcans. Eventually, they too were defeated. Throughout its history, pirates had made Majorca a favorite base of operations, attracted by the myriad inlets and coves that dotted its shoreline. From there, they would launch forays against commercial shipping in the Mediterranean, which was Europe's economic lifeline, or simply plunder the island's many prosperous villages. The stone watchtowers that guarded the island's coast stood in testimony to the frequency and cost of these sea wolves' depredations.

Several leagues from the sea, between the mountain ranges, lies Majorca's central plain, a fertile region well suited to agriculture. Here, most of the island's rich produce is grown—olives, figs, almonds, apricots, oranges, grapes, lemons, pomegranates, plums, melons, and pimentos as well as cereals and vegetables—in well-tended orchards and arbors and in terraced fields divided by stone walls. On the edges of this plain are the island's most important agricultural villages and cities—Inca, La Puebla, Alaro, Manacor, Felanitx, and Petra.

A view of the rocky coast of Majorca, near the fishing village of Deyá. Throughout the island's history, Majorcans made their living from the sea. At the same time, they were forced to defend themselves against invaders from foreign lands and pirates who wished to use Majorca as a base of operations.

At the beginning of the 18th century, Petra, called the Nest of Majorca, had 2,000 inhabitants, most of whom lived in low stone houses covered with slightly angled roofs of brown, orange, and amber tile. Here, at 1:00 A.M. on November 24, 1713, a son was born to Antonio and Margarita Serra. In the stillness of the night immediately following the birth, the proud father nailed a laurel branch to the wooden front door of the family home on Calle Barracar; this was the way of announcing to friends and neighbors that the family had been blessed with the birth of a baby boy. As darkness gave way to dawn a few hours later, the midwife took the child from his mother, who had given birth in a small loft on the second floor of the Serra home. In the arms of the midwife, who led a procession consisting of the godparents, the father, and other friends and relatives who would figure prominently in his life, the newborn infant was carried two blocks to Calle Mayor and the Church of San Pedro, where he was baptized Miguel José Serra.

The baby was Antonio and Margarita's third child; both of the others had died before receiving the sacrament of baptism, which in Catholic belief purifies the recipient of original sin. This time, the Serras were taking no chances. After the ceremony, the midwife returned the child to his mother with the joyous announcement,

"We return your son to you a Christian." While mother and son rested in the small room above, downstairs the baby's godparents hosted the traditional party in the main room of the house, dispensing sweets and the exquisite Majorcan brandy. Several weeks later, when Margarita had regained her strength, father and mother carried their son, swaddled in blankets against December's chill, to the hillside shrine of Nuestra Señora de Bon Any (Our Lady of the Good Year in the Majorcan dialect, which is more closely akin to Catalan than to Spanish), as Mary, the mother of Christ, was revered by the Petrans. The Señora de Bon Any was the patron saint and guardian of Petra; inhabitants of the village made the pilgrimage to her shrine, more than 1,000 feet above the village, to ask for success in some venture dear to their heart, to pray for a loved one, or most important—after laying an offering of crops at her feet—to ask that the Señora provide them with a successful harvest in the year to come.

After a brief ceremony, Antonio and Margarita symbolically entrusted their most precious gift—the tiny, slumbering infant Miguel—to the benevolent protection of Nuestra Señora de Bon Any. Months later, when the baby was ready to walk, his proud

The coat of arms of the village of Petra, Serra's birthplace. When Margarita Serra gave birth to her third child, her husband, Antonio, nailed a laurel branch to the door of the family's simple stone house. This was the traditional way of announcing the birth of a baby boy to friends and neighbors.

parents took him to a different incarnation of the Virgin Mary—the white-and-gold image of Nuestra Señora de los Angeles (Our Lady of the Angels)—where the children of Petra were coaxed into taking their first tentative steps so that in life they would always walk in the protection of the Virgin.

Like most of the residents of Petra, the Serras were peasant farmers. Both men and women worked in the fields, which were quite distant from the village. Each morning at dawn the Petrans left for the day's work. Carrying their tools, several generations of a family—parents, grandparents, and grandchildren—rode to the fields on a cart pulled by the family donkey. Everyone, including the children, was expected to join in the work. It was exhausting labor, lasting from sunup to sundown and even later on nights when the full moon shone. Majorca's climate was temperate and gentle, but it still took much hard work and ingenuity to coax from the rocky soil of the central plain the bounteous harvests for which the islanders were famous. And there was the constant worry shared by agricultural peoples the world over: Would there be enough rain? Majorca's fields, orchards, arbors, and groves were cleverly terraced to aid in irrigation, but such methods also caused erosion and thus could not be overused. The roofs of the large landowners' castles were engineered in a system of complicated, interrelated terraces that collected whatever rain fell and conducted it to cisterns for storage and future use. The peasants more commonly relied on the intercession of the Señora de Bon Any.

At day's end, the Serras' weary donkey trudged slowly back from the fields to Petra, pulling the cart that carried the family and their tools. The Serra home was a two-story stone structure, fronted by an arched wooden doorway, with a small, walled garden in back. The door opened onto the main room, or parlor, which like the rest of the house was painted white and contained a few pieces of simple wooden furniture. While Antonio stabled the donkey in its stall next to the kitchen, Margarita prepared supper by the light of an oil lamp. The staple foods of Majorcan peasants such as the

Serras were beans, cheese, fruits, vegetables, and bread made from wheat. *Enseimada*, the sweet Majorcan cake, was a special treat. After the meal, there was barely enough time for some casual conversation before exhaustion carried everyone off to sleep. Only on Sunday, which was devoted to worship, rest, and relaxation, and holy days, such as Christmas and Easter, was there a break in the endless cycle of planting, tending, and harvesting.

Like most Majorcans, the Serras were devout Catholics. Their faith was not restricted to once-a-week attendance at Sunday mass but was the most vital component of their life, informing virtually everything that they did. Time was measured by the church calendar, which divided the entire year into feast days and occasions for observances; prayers were said upon awaking, before retiring at night, and before each meal. Religion gave meaning to a life that otherwise might have been seen as an unending, unprofitable, backbreaking attempt to wrest a modest subsistence from an indifferent earth. But to the Serras and other Majorcans, the evidence of God's goodness and generosity was everywhere—in the magnificent sun that summoned them to work each day, seemingly rising out of the Mediterranean's pale blue waters; in the gentle breeze that moved the island's windmills; in the poppies and wildflowers that ran riot on the hillsides outside of Petra; in the unexpected afternoon shower that watered the thirsty crops and refreshed the tired workers; in the bread and wine they partook of in the shade at noontime, so delicious and reviving after a morning's work; in the grapes ripening on the vines and the wheat rippling in the fields at the autumn harvest; in the fruit and grain drying upstairs in the storage room during the winter months.

With so much work to be done, there was little thought of sending young Miguel to school. Like the other youths of Petra, he was needed in the fields to hoe, to weed, to tend the livestock, to fetch water from the town cistern. When he was not in the fields, often as not Miguel could be found with the friars at the Franciscan Church and Convent of San Bernardino, just a few hundred yards

A typical Majorcan landscape, near the town of Sóller. Though the Serras struggled to make a living from the soil, their religion taught them to be thankful for what they had and for the beauty of their native island.

from the Serra home. The priests there were always glad to see Miguel, a boy of unusual good cheer and curiosity. He would wander in alone and ask one of the priests to read him a story from *The Little Flowers of St. Francis*, a collection of stories portraying the good works of Francis of Assisi. St. Francis was a great lover of animals, and Miguel especially enjoyed those episodes in which the saint preached to the birds and the beasts of the forest. As a young man, St. Francis had been quite wealthy, but he had renounced all of his earthly riches in order to follow Christ, and he required his followers to take a vow of poverty. This also greatly impressed the young boy.

The Franciscans at San Bernardino were equally impressed with the intelligence exhibited by young Miguel, and several of them took upon themselves the responsibility of providing him with an education. He quickly learned to read and write and was

soon taking lessons in Latin. With his parents' consent, he began
spending more and more time at the convent. His gift for music,
particularly Gregorian chant (the unharmonized chant that is
the liturgical music of the Roman Catholic church), was so pronounced that he was allowed to become a member of the adult
choir. He also learned mathematics and theology, and he spent
much time in devotional exercises in the convent's 13 ornately
decorated chapels, each one dedicated to a martyred saint.

Over time, it became clear that Miguel was a rare boy, in both
his intellectual potential and the depths of his faith. Pleased by his
talent and devotion, Antonio and Margarita arranged for Miguel's
further education and development to be placed under the care
of a priest at the cathedral in Palma. Accordingly, when Miguel
was about 15, he and his parents made the long trip by donkey to
the capital city, which was some 25 miles away on a deep bay on the
southwestern coast of the island.

*This view of Palma features the Lonja, the city's commercial exchange, in the center,
with the great cathedral to the right. The capital city was a far more challenging
environment than the little town of Petra, and it stimulated the young Serra to
pursue his vocation as a priest.*

The capital, then a city of 30,000 people, was quite a contrast to sleepy Petra. Petra had nothing remotely resembling Palma's great cathedral, built on the site of a Moorish mosque, or the Lonja, the architectural pride of Majorca, a magnificent edifice housing the city's commercial exchange. Palma was also home to a great university, dedicated to the memory of Ramon Llull, the Catalan mystic, philosopher, and poet who lived in Majorca during the 13th century before becoming a missionary in Asia and Africa. Still, it did not take Miguel long to make his mark. After a year of study at the cathedral, he enrolled as a student of philosophy at another Franciscan institution, the Convent of San Francisco, which prepared religiously inclined students for the priesthood and secular youths for a variety of professions. By this time, Miguel was quite certain of his vocation and was determined to become a Franciscan priest, but his first application was rejected because of his small stature and youthful, somewhat frail appearance. Only a special petition by his instructors enabled him to begin his novitiate at the Franciscan Convent of Jesus, outside the city walls, in 1730.

The novitiate is a period of contemplation and seclusion, often a year in length, during which the candidate and the elder members of the community attempt to determine the authenticity of his vocation. Miguel was denied letters and visitors during this period as he struggled to decide whether he was indeed willing to devote his entire life to God. His days were filled with prayers, silence, meditation, and routine physical chores, but at the conclusion of the novitiate he was more eager than ever to take the vows of poverty, chastity, and obedience and become a full-fledged member of the Franciscan community. On September 15, 1731, he did so, taking as his religious name Junípero, after the sometimes buffoonish but always faithful companion of St. Francis, who praised Junípero's childlike simplicity and compassion as the epitome of Christian charity. The original Junípero was known as the Jester of God and often had to be stopped lest he literally give the robe off his back and the sandals from his feet to those less fortunate than himself. Junípero Serra saw in his namesake's devotion and delightful good humor ideals to which he could aspire.

After taking his vows, Serra returned to the Convent and Church of San Francisco, a huge gothic structure dating from the 13th century. Here, he began a new round of studies in preparation for his ordination as a priest and what he expected to be his life's work as a professor. Three years of study in philosophy were followed by intensive training in theology, including courses in logic, dialectics, metaphysics, and cosmology. Along the way, he was ordained subdeacon (on December 18, 1734) and deacon (on March 17, 1736), steps preparatory to final ordination as a priest. Those of Serra's classmates who had endured the long intellectual and spiritual ordeal were ordained priests on May 31, 1737. But Serra was not among them—not because of any doubts about his fitness as a priest but because his rapid progress and superior abilities had brought him to the verge of priesthood before his 24th birthday, the minimum age at which a member of the Franciscan order could be ordained.

There were no such restrictions, however, on the age at which a Franciscan could put his intellectual abilities to use as a teacher. Even though he was not yet ordained, Serra was asked to sit for the competitive examinations from which new professors would be chosen. This was a singular recognition of his talents on the part of his instructors, and Serra did not disappoint them. In late November 1737, after several days of grueling oral exams, Serra received notice that he had been unanimously chosen to become the new lector of philosophy, as soon as a position was available. His ordination as a priest followed soon thereafter, sometime during the Advent season, as the four weeks before Christmas are known in the Catholic calendar.

All who knew Junípero Serra expected him to enjoy a distinguished career as a teacher and intellectual. As an instructor at the Convent of San Francisco he was much admired, particularly by two students who would later occupy an important place in his life,

St. Francis of Assisi founded the Order of St. Francis in Italy in 1209. When Miguel Serra joined the order in 1731, he took the name of Junípero, who had been a close companion of St. Francis's. Serra hoped to emulate the simplicity, charity, and good humor of both men.

Francisco Palóu and Juan Crespí. Later, Palóu would become Serra's closest friend and the author of a massive biography of him that is the primary source of material about his life. Crespí would win fame as the missionary explorer and chronicler of the Spanish settlement of California, a process in which Serra would be the driving force.

In addition to his duties as a teacher, Serra served as the convent's librarian—a post restricted to individuals of proven scholarly achievement—and continued his own studies in sacred theology at the University of Ramon Llull (sometimes referred to as the University of Palma). He received his doctorate in 1742 and less than a year later was asked to fill the chair in sacred theology at the university. The chair was named after Duns Scotus, the 13th-century Scottish Franciscan who attempted to prove a synthesis, or union, between reason and faith. Serra's own attempts at synthesis were demonstrated by his ability to propose sophisticated philosophical proofs of the existence of God when teaching in the university and to preach moving lessons, understandable by even the most uneducated peasant, in the frequent sermons he gave around Majorca.

Palóu wrote that "Serra's sermons were received with applause not only by the lettered but by the unlettered. Sprung from the country soil of Petra himself, Serra never lost the ability to touch his simple hearers." In 1743, Serra was awarded the honor of giving the annual sermon in the cathedral on the Feast of Corpus Christi, for which only the most talented orators were chosen, and for the next six years he continued to preach his fiery sermons all over the island. His words were always received enthusiastically, perhaps because at this time the faith of the people of Majorca needed bolstering. The years between 1743 and 1749 were a period of drought and plague on the island, and both people and crops suffered greatly.

During one of his visits to Petra, which were never as frequent as he would have liked, Serra found his father deathly ill and expressed remorse over the course that had taken him from his family. Antonio, who eventually recovered, told him that his only responsibility was to God. "My son," he said, "let me charge you to be a good religious [a member of a monastic order] of your Father, Saint Francis."

Serra's reputation continued to grow. Sometime in 1748, he received word that he had been chosen to give the sermon on the feast day honoring Ramon Llull. This lesson was to be given in the great cathedral, beneath the tilted sarcophagus, or stone coffin, that held the remains of the university's patron saint; to be asked to preach on this occasion was the greatest honor that a Majorcan priest could receive. But Serra's joy at this accolade was tempered by the crisis he was now undergoing, for all his academic and intellectual successes were beginning to feel hollow and meaningless to him.

He had started to feel that the Lord's greatest work was done by the missionaries—by those who toiled in the spiritual vineyards, as it were, as opposed to those academics who concerned themselves with abstract doctrines, philosophical quandaries, and the endless dialectic between reason and faith. He now engaged himself in a new debate and resolved to go to Mexico—leaving behind family, friends, and his well-earned reputation—to serve as a missionary to the Indians, who would scarce be able to appreciate his eloquence and learning. When the second message came from Mezquía, informing Serra that there were indeed berths available on the ship that was to carry the missionaries to Mexico City, he sent word that he would fill one of the spots. The sermon he preached in the cathedral on January 25, 1749, reflected all the pent-up fervor of his new commitment, the energy of the argument he had conducted with himself, and the surety of the new peace he had found in making his decision. No record exists of the words Serra spoke that day, only the comment of one of his fellow learned professors: "This sermon is worthy of being printed in letters of gold."

CHRISTOFEL COLONUS

Christopher Columbus established the Spanish presence in the New World with his daring voyage to the Caribbean in 1492. He also began the European tradition of exploiting and maltreating the native inhabitants, whom he described as "wonderfully timorous" and "fit to be ordered about and made to work."

CHAPTER THREE

The Sword and the Cross

By the time Serra decided to become a missionary, Spain had already maintained a New World empire of astonishing dimensions and wealth for more than 250 years. The Spanish presence in the Americas began with Christopher Columbus's landfall on the tiny island in the Caribbean, not far east of present-day Florida, that he called San Salvador and that the Indians knew as Guanahaní. There, on a sandy beach whose exact location is still a subject of historical debate, the peoples of the Old and New Worlds first encountered one another. For Columbus, the meeting was somewhat disappointing. He had not expected or wished to discover the gateway to two new continents previously unknown to Europeans. He had begun with the conviction that by sailing west across the Atlantic, he would succeed in reaching the Indies (the name by which China, India, and nearby Asian lands and regions were known to Europeans). In so doing, he hoped to make available Asia's riches—primarily spices, which included perfumes and medicines as well as preservatives and flavor enhancers, such as pepper and cinnamon—to European exploitation. Europeans had been searching for a sea route to the Far East ever since the Ottoman Turks had closed the Levant, through which Asian goods traveled on their way to Mediterranean seaports, to Christians.

But instead of the fabled jewel-encrusted palace of the Great Khan, as Europeans were in the habit of referring to China's emperor, Columbus found on San Salvador a small number of naked men and women. They were members of the Taino tribe of the Arawak language group. These natives were "very well-built, of very handsome bodies and very fine faces," Columbus observed, but they gave no evidence of being the subjects of a wealthy and powerful ruler. Still, Columbus thought that his discovery, whatever it was—he called the natives Indios in the belief, or hope, that he had indeed reached the Indies—could profit himself and the Crown. These Indians, Columbus wrote in a letter to Ferdinand and Isabella, Spain's monarchs, "are so artless and so free with all they possess, that no one would believe it without having seen it. Of anything they have, if you ask them for it, they never say no; rather they invite the person to share it, and show as much love as if they were giving their hearts; and whether the thing be of value or of small price, at once they are content with whatever little thing of whatever kind may be given to them." Even better, Columbus wrote, the Indians posed absolutely no danger to the Spanish and were unable to defend their territory. He described them as "wonderfully timorous" and unwilling to use weapons. This timidity meant "that with 50 armed men these people could be brought under control and made to do whatever one might wish." In his log, Columbus was even more explicit: "[The Indians are] very cowardly, . . . fit to be ordered about and made to work, to sow and do [whatever] else that may be needed." In other words, the Indians would make good slaves. "How easy it would be," Columbus wrote, "to convert these people—and to make them work for us."

Because of the poverty of its inhabitants, San Salvador did not interest Columbus all that much, but he soon found another island that did. "Hispaniola is marvelous," Columbus wrote. He described the island as lush, possessing abundant water, blessed with thickly timbered mountains and fertile plains "so beautiful and so fat for planting and sowing, and for livestock of every sort, and for building towns and cities." The Indians there were as "wonderfully timorous" as were the inhabitants of San Salvador, and more important, they had plenty of gold and other precious metals. Leaving behind a garrison force in a fortress constructed from the timbers of his wrecked flagship, the *Santa María*, Columbus sailed for Spain from Hispaniola in January 1493 to inform Ferdinand and Isabella of his finds.

Columbus's discovery came at an extremely propitious time for Spain. On January 2, 1492, Ferdinand and Isabella had accepted the surrender of the Moorish sultan Muhammad XI, known to the Spanish as Boabdil, on a field outside of the besieged Moorish city of Granada, in southern Spain. When Los Reyes Católicos (the Catholic Monarchs, an honorary title bestowed on them by a grateful papacy for their service to Christendom) seated themselves on the throne in the Alhambra, the magnificent palace of Granada's Moorish rulers, it marked an end to more than 800 years of battle between the Moors and the Spanish on the Iberian Peninsula. Granada had been the last stronghold in Spain of the Moors, who had once ruled most of the peninsula; with the end of the Reconquista (Reconquest), Ferdinand and Isabella were finally poised to unite the disparate kingdoms and provinces of Spain into a nation. They also now had time and energy to devote to other affairs. One of their first acts was to approve the expenditure of funds to finance Columbus's proposed voyage in search of a western passage to the Indies, a proposition that they had been considering for several years but had been unable to act upon because of the ongoing conflict.

The end of the Reconquista also meant that Spain had the resources and the will necessary to exploit Columbus's discoveries. Generations of warfare had bred in Spain some of Europe's most

Spanish conquistadores plunder a pile of gold captured from the Aztec. The desire for wealth impelled many Spaniards to set sail for the New World. "We Spanish suffer from a disease of the heart which can only be cured by gold," wrote Hernán Cortés, the conqueror of Mexico.

ferocious fighting men, accustomed to hardship and adventure, willing to sacrifice their lives in defense of their Catholic religion. They had been raised to believe that Catholicism was the one true faith, and their victory over the Muslim Moors was taken as proof of divine favor. For much of the Spanish nobility, conquest and battle were the accepted means of proving oneself; for members of the lower classes, military service was a means of getting ahead. Moreover, the Reconquista had left Spain economically devastated, with even much of its nobility landless and impoverished. Columbus's new world offered Spain's men of fighting age three opportunities that they coveted—to attain glory, to serve God, and to find gold.

Columbus's second voyage, which departed Spain in September 1493, was thus equipped for conquest and colonization. This time, instead of 3 tiny vessels, the bold Admiral of the Ocean Sea commanded a flotilla of 17 ships, manned by 1,200 would-be colonists, the great majority of them soldiers and *hidalgos* (Spanish noblemen) who had volunteered in the hope of making their fortune in the New World. Also on board were a number of large dogs intended to be used to terrorize any Indians who would not cooperate, and six priests, who intended to convert the natives.

Upon arriving on Hispaniola, Columbus discovered that the Indians of the New World were not quite as timid as he might have expected. The garrison he had left behind at Navidad, as he had named the fortress, had been slaughtered by the Indians, who had not put up for long with the Spaniards' depredations, which included pressing the natives into slavery and raping their women. But the Spanish had come to stay, and they quickly established control of the island and built several settlements. Columbus himself led several military thrusts against the Indians. The monarchs eventually replaced Columbus as viceroy and governor of Hispaniola because of the excesses of his dictatorial rule. (They were more concerned, however, with his offenses against their Spanish subjects than with his mistreatment of the Indians.)

Although there was much grumbling in Spain because Hispaniola, contrary to Columbus's claims, did not contain enough gold to make everyone rich within a year, the Spanish continued to venture to the New World. In addition to soldiers, pigs, horses, cattle, and Catholicism, the Spanish brought to the New World germs to which the Indians had never developed immunity, as they had never been exposed to them before. These germs, the smallpox virus chief among them, were as effective as guns and ammunition in bringing about the Spanish conquest. Those Indians the Spanish did not hunt down and kill or enslave were wiped out by disease; by the middle of the 16th century, the Indian population on Hispaniola, estimated at about 50,000 at the time of Columbus's arrival, had been reduced to nothing.

When the Spanish had exhausted Hispaniola's gold deposits, they looked for new conquests. On April 21, 1519, a 34-year-old conquistador named Hernán Cortés landed his fleet of 10 ships, manned by 508 soldiers, at a beautiful natural harbor on the southeast coast of Mexico. There, he founded a new settlement, Veracruz (True Cross), and destroyed his ships on the beach in order to forcefully impress upon his men that there was no turning back. Cortés had been a law student in Spain, but like so many members of the Spanish upper class he had come to the New

Hernán Cortés (1485–1547), shown kneeling before the king of Spain, landed at Veracruz on the coast of Mexico in 1519 with barely more than 500 soldiers. In little more than a year, this small force succeeded in toppling the mighty Aztec Empire. The Spaniards were aided by superior weapons, clever strategy, and diseases that ravaged the Indian population.

World to seek his fortune. He distinguished himself in the conquest of Cuba and became one of the richest and most powerful men on the island. But when news arrived of an extremely wealthy province of Mexico known as the Yucatán, he resolved to sail in search of it, despite explicit orders from Cuba's governor prohibiting him from doing so. "We Spanish suffer from a disease of the heart which can only be cured by gold," Cortés wrote by way of explaining his motivation.

At the head of his small force, Cortés marched for the interior. Although always greatly outnumbered, he won a series of victories over the Indians, whose courage was no match for the guns and cannons of the Spanish. For the Indians, the horses that Cortés and some of his men rode were even more terrifying than the weapons that so easily killed them. Horses are not native to the New World; some of the Indians believed that each horse and rider was actually one terrible creature that shot fire from the magic stick it carried. Many of the defeated Indians joined forces with the powerful newcomers, who disclosed through an interpreter, a Mayan Indian woman who became known as Dótno Malinche, their intention of marching on Tenochtitlán.

Built on the site of present-day Mexico City, 200 miles west of Veracruz, Tenochtitlán was the magnificent capital city of the empire of the Aztec, who held the other Indian peoples of Mexico in thrall. Inhabited by perhaps 500,000 people—Paris at the time was home to 65,000 people; London, to 40,000—it more than matched in splendor and opulence any city in Europe. The Spanish, when they arrived, were as awestruck by the riches to be found in Tenochtitlán as they were appalled by the bloodiness of the Aztec religion, in which human sacrifice played a central role.

Reports of the terrible invaders, with their fearsome animals and awful weapons, had reached Tenochtitlán and the Aztec emperor, Montezuma II, long before Cortés set foot in the city. To Montezuma and the Aztec, the arrival of Cortés and his men could mean only one thing—the reappearance of their departed god, Quetzalcoatl, who according to their religion was destined to return from the east. Everything they had heard about the newcomers—their prowess in battle, their magical weapons and

A 16th-century engraving shows Aztec women seeking the protection of their ruler, Montezuma II, after their husbands had fallen in battle with Spanish soldiers. The conquerors' terrifying horses and fire-spewing weapons helped to convince the Aztec that the invading Spaniards were the ancient gods returning to rule them.

animals—only convinced the Aztec that the Spanish were gods. An omen in the sky even heralded their coming: According to an Aztec legend later recorded by Spanish missionaries, "It was like a flaming ear of corn, or a fiery signal, or the blaze of daybreak; it seemed to bleed fire, drop by drop, like a wound from the sky."

Accordingly, the Aztec welcomed Cortés and his men, and Montezuma soon became in effect a hostage puppet ruler, used by the Spanish to pacify the population while they looted the city. Eventually, the Aztec rebelled and drove the invaders away on June 30, 1520, an event the Spanish called Triste Noche (Sad Night). But Cortés, reinforced by new arrivals from Cuba, was able to regroup his forces and carry out a brilliantly conceived assault that left the Spanish in control of Tenochtitlán and ultimately the vast and inconceivably wealthy Aztec Empire. (Ironically, Cortés's reinforcements had been sent from Cuba to compel him to return, but his descriptions of Aztec gold and silver convinced them to cast their lot with him.) Tenochtitlán was torn down, stone by stone, until nothing of it remained; 300,000 of its citizens perished in the Spanish siege.

Cortés's conquest was more immediately appreciated by the Spanish crown than Columbus's had been, perhaps because it yielded greater instant dividends, in the form of gold and silver. By 1530, the Crown's traditional one-fifth share of all the precious metals mined in the New World amounted to the modern-day equivalent of $2 million annually, a simply enormous sum for the era. It enabled Ferdinand's successors on the throne, Charles I and Philip II, to become the most powerful monarchs in Europe. The New World's wealth also made Cortés and countless other conquistadores fabulously wealthy. Cortés's personal estate stretched from the Atlantic to the Pacific, occupying one-quarter of the present-day nation of Mexico; it contained 22 separate villages, 23,000 Indian slaves, and countless gold and silver mines. Even so, he was not satisfied; he led further expeditions of exploration and conquest to Honduras and Baja California. "The lust for glory

Conquistadores in Peru receiving the blessing of priests. In addition to seeking gold and glory, the Spaniards were determined to convert the Indians to Catholicism. Both the soldiers and the missionaries believed that they were serving God by spreading the true faith in the New World.

extends beyond this mortal life, and taking a whole world will hardly satisfy it, much less one or two kingdoms," he wrote.

Before and after Cortés's victory over the Aztec, conquistadores flocked to the New World. In many instances, the Crown did not even have to pay for its conquests. Would-be conquistadores were expected to foot the bill for their expeditions in the New World, in exchange for the right to govern or economically exploit whatever land they could conquer and defend. On its part, the Crown demanded only its customary one-fifth. Vasco Núñez de Balboa crossed the isthmus of Panama and "discovered" the Pacific Ocean in 1513, the same year that Juan Ponce de León landed in Florida. Pánfilo de Narváez led a disastrous colonizing effort in Florida in the late 1520s; a shipwrecked member of that expedition, Álvar Núñez Cabeza de Vaca, walked from the Gulf of Mexico near present-day Galveston, Texas, to the Gulf of California. In the middle of the same decade, with a comparative handful of men, Francisco Pizarro conquered the empire of the Incas, which was every bit as advanced and wealthy as that of the Aztec and stretched virtually the entire cordillera of the Andes along the Pacific coast of South America. Like Cortés, Pizarro benefited from the Indians' belief that he and his men had supernatural powers as well as from superior technology and the Indians' fear of horses. From 1539 to 1542, Hernando de Soto led 600 soldiers, 200 horses, a pack of ravening dogs, and a herd of voracious hogs on a murderous trek that took them from Florida through much of the present-day American South and beyond the Mississippi.

At almost the same time, Francisco Vásquez de Coronado was departing from near the mouth of the Gulf of California at the head of an expedition charged with finding the storied Seven Cities of Cibola, which were supposedly "large and powerful villages, four and five stories high." The cities were in fact the settlements of the Pueblo Indians, and because they contained no gold, Coronado found them disappointing. Still, in the course of his wanderings he became the first European to explore present-day Arizona and New Mexico, and he even got as far as the plains of Oklahoma and Texas. Together, these conquistadores and countless others like them gave Spain, by virtue of conquest and first discovery (the presence of the Indians irregardless), claims to a vast American empire.

Its martial prowess notwithstanding, Spain used more than military might to subdue the Americas. Its greatest asset was the presence of its people on American shores. As was true in the Caribbean, the diseases the Spanish brought with them did much more to devastate the native inhabitants than force of arms or slavery ever could. As the historian Francis Jennings has pointed out, just shaking hands with a Spaniard could be a biological trauma for the immunologically unprotected Indians: "Not even the most brutally depraved of the conquistadors was able purposely to slaughter Indians on the scale that the gentle priest unwittingly accomplished by going from his sickbed ministrations to lay his hands in blessing on his Indian converts." Within a century of Cortés's conquest, the Indian population in central Mexico had been reduced from 25 million to 2 million, largely through the ravages of smallpox and other diseases. The same sort of decline occurred in other areas of New Spain and indeed everywhere in the Americas where Europeans came into contact with the Indians.

Spain used the cross as well as the sword to conquer the Indians. Catholic missionaries were among the first European inhabitants of the New World. Six priests sailed with Columbus on his second voyage, and when the first Franciscan missionaries landed on Mexican shores in 1523, Cortés, that battle-hardened, rapacious conquistador, knelt and kissed the hems of their gray robes. Although Christian ideals would seem to be at odds with the harsh treatment the Indians received, it must be remembered that

Illustrations from a 17th-century book show some of the cruelties inflicted on the Indians by their Spanish conquerors. Even more devastating were the diseases brought by the Europeans: By the beginning of the 17th century, the native population of Mexico had been reduced from 25 million to 2 million.

Spanish Catholicism in the 16th century, as shaped by hundreds of years of warfare with the Muslims, was an extremely militant faith. The conquistador and the missionary were both likely to believe that they were doing the natives of the New World a service by bringing them the one true faith, although the missionary's methods were apt to be gentler.

For the Crown, the men of the cloth were nearly as important as the soldiers, for it was easier, and less expensive, to govern a pacified population than to be constantly at war. The Crown therefore encouraged the development in the New World of missions, which were essentially settlements in Indian territory where priests (and in some cases nuns) could live close to the Indians and attempt to convert them to Catholicism. Such conversions implied more than a mere profession of faith, however; it meant renouncing the Indian way of life for the "civilized" habits more suitable for Spanish purposes. The Indians had to leave their native lands and villages, settle in areas controlled by the missions, and adopt the life of the peasant agricultural laborer. Very often, conversion meant the renunciation of life itself because the missions were often centers for the transmission of disease.

Although the missionary system certainly played a large role in the Spanish conquest and in the destruction of the Indian way of life, the men and women who volunteered as missionaries acted for the most part out of a genuine religious conviction. They were certain that they were working for the ultimate benefit of the Indians. Unlike the conquistadores, few missionaries profited personally from their actions, although they shared many of the same risks, most notably death in a strange, far-off land. They were certainly individuals of exceptional courage, for many of the missions in Mexico were established in regions where the conquistadores had been unable to quell the natives or where they had not yet ventured. Over time, the Crown came to prefer using missionaries and missions, rather than soldiers, to extend New Spain's frontiers.

Bartolomé de Las Casas (1474–1566) came to Hispaniola as a plantation owner and became the first priest ordained in the New World. In 1530, Las Casas persuaded the king of Spain to abolish slavery in Peru. Despite his efforts, laws protecting the Indians were often disregarded by the soldiers.

Some missionaries came to genuinely love and care for the Indians. Although the relocation of the Indians to mission settlements often took place at the point of a bayonet, and although few missionaries shied away from using whippings, imprisonment, and the destruction of Indian temples to hasten the process of conversion, the priests of the New World sometimes sided with the Indians, even when to do so placed them in opposition to the Crown or to the colonial government. Bartolomé de Las Casas, for example, the revered "apostle to the Indies" who was the first priest ordained in the New World, used his writings and influence to draw attention to the horrible mistreatment of the Indians; in 1544 he succeeded in getting slavery abolished in Peru. Jesuit missionaries in Paraguay and southwestern Brazil were such fierce opponents of slavery and defenders of the rights of the Indians under their care that those regions were sometimes said to constitute a separate Jesuit kingdom within New Spain.

By 1749, when Junípero Serra volunteered to take a missionary post in Mexico, the mission system was an established and integral part of New Spain. But Spain's glory was the Indians' ruin, and the Indians continued to resist adopting Spanish civilization in perhaps the only way remaining to them: They died.

The bustling seaport of Cádiz forms the backdrop in this painting by Francisco de Zurbarán. In 1749, Fathers Serra and Palóu spent four months in Cádiz, preparing for the journey to Mexico. Before leaving, Serra wrote a long letter explaining his departure to his parents.

CHAPTER FOUR

The Camino Real

Serra and Palóu set sail from Palma for the Spanish port of Málaga on April 13, 1749. Before doing so, Serra paid a farewell visit to Petra, but he could not bring himself to actually say good-bye to his aged parents. Antonio was now 73, and Margarita was 71, a ripe old age for the time and place; both would have realized, had their son told them of his plans, that in all likelihood they would never set eyes on him again. The thought greatly troubled Serra, but he kept in mind Christ's teaching—"Anyone who prefers father or mother to me is not worthy of me"—and remained silent about his imminent departure, fearing that his parents would beg him not to go and that he would succumb to their entreaties.

Serra and Palóu survived the 15-day journey to Málaga in good health, despite the menacings of their English captain, a Protestant—an "obstinate heretic," according to Palóu—whose wrath Serra earned by repeatedly besting him in disputes on religious subjects. Several times, the captain threatened to throw the priests overboard, and at one point he even drew his dagger and held it at Serra's throat before stalking off in a rage. Serra and Palóu were grateful to reach Málaga, where they stayed for several weeks at the Convent of San Luis before making another brief sea journey to Cádiz, the *Villasota*'s port of embarkation for the New World.

It took four months for the *Villasota* to be made ready for departure. During that time, Serra rested and prepared himself at the Convent of San Francisco, where he also helped with the spiritual duties of the Franciscan community in residence there. A document later discovered in missionary archives in Seville described Serra at the time as being "of medium height [he was, however, no more than five-foot-two], swarthy, dark eyes and hair, scant beard." Although short and slight, Serra possessed a wiry strength, the legacy of his childhood days in the fields, and his stamina and capacity for self-denial always astounded his colleagues. He normally slept only between the hours of 8:00 P.M. and midnight and then arose to pray until dawn. He ate sparingly and rarely consumed meat, taking almost literally the Franciscan directive to depend on "the table of the Lord," or God's providence. Serra believed that his religious vocation had made him physically robust: "In the novitiate, I was almost always ill and so small of stature that I was unable to reach the lectern, nor could I help my fellow novices in the necessary chores of the novitiate. Therefore, the Father Master of Novices employed me solely in serving Mass daily. However, with my profession I gained health and strength and grew to medium size. I attribute all this to my profession, for which I give infinite thanks to God."

Unlike the five Franciscans who had changed their mind about going to the New World, Serra did not allow his first look at the waves of the Atlantic to shake his determination. But he continued to think about all that he would be leaving behind, particularly his aging parents. He wrote them a long letter in which he attempted to explain his actions, addressing it to Francisco Serra (no relation), a trusted friend and fellow priest at the Convent of San Bernardino in his hometown, with instructions that it should be read to his family only after the *Villasota* had sailed. In the letter, Serra spoke of the mixed feelings of joy and sorrow with which he departed: "Words cannot express the feelings of my heart as I bid you farewell nor can I properly repeat to you my request that you be the consolation of my parents to sustain them in their sorrow. I wish I could communicate to them the great joy that fills my heart. If I could do this, then surely they would encourage me to go forward and never to turn back. Let them remember that the office of an apostolic preacher [a missionary], especially in its actual exercise, is the greatest calling to which they could wish me to be chosen."

He asked Francisco Serra to remind his parents, in their anguish, that it was their faith and devotion that first inspired him with the love of God, and he urged them to realize that in performing God's work he was ensuring the greatest ultimate happiness both for himself and for them:

> Tell them that I shall ever feel the loss of not being able to be near them as heretofore to console them, but since first things must come first and before all else, the first thing to do is to fulfill the will of God. It was for the love of God that I left them and if I, for the love of God and with the aid of His grace, had the strength of will to do so, it will be to the point that they too, for the love of God, be content to be deprived of my company. . . . Let them rejoice that they have a son who is a priest, though an unworthy one and a sinner, who daily in the holy sacrifice of the Mass prays for them with all the fervor of his soul and many days applies the Mass for them alone, so that the Lord may aid them; that they may not lack their daily bread, that He may give them patience in their trials, resignation to His holy will, peace and union with everyone, courage to fight the temptations of the evil one, and last of all, when it is God's will, a tranquil death in His holy grace. If I, by the grace of God, succeed in becoming a good religious, my prayers will become more efficacious, and they in consequence will be the gainers.

Serra departed for Mexico from Cádiz aboard the *Villasota* on August 30, 1749. The voyage to Puerto Rico, where the ship was scheduled to stop for reprovisioning and maintenance, took about five weeks, slightly longer than expected, which resulted in some shortages of supplies, particularly fresh drinking water. On the latter stages of the journey, the captain was forced to ration water to about a half-pint per day for each passenger. Serra bore this inconvenience uncomplainingly, with his customary asceticism, advising his colleagues that he found that he was less thirsty if he ate and talked less, although he later confided in writing that "there were moments when my throat was burning so that I would not have hesitated to drink from the dirtiest puddle in the road." During a stopover of 18 days in San Juan, the capital city of Puerto Rico founded by Ponce de León in 1508, Serra and his fellow missionaries preached several sermons and sometimes heard confessions around the clock. From Puerto Rico, the ship continued westward through the maze of islands that dot the Caribbean, finally landing at Veracruz on December 6. All of the missionaries but Serra disembarked in various stages of illness; some, like Palóu, were so sick that it was feared they would die.

Mexico City and the Apostolic College of San Fernando were 200 miles west of Veracruz. The king of Spain, Charles III, had ordered that horses be provided to transport the newcomers, but Serra preferred to make his way on foot, as a true *fraile andariego*, or walking friar. In this he was emulating other Franciscan missionaries, such as St. Francis Solano, who had already distinguished themselves in the New World. Besides, the official rules of the Franciscan order, in keeping with its collective vow of poverty, required that a member "must not ride on horseback unless compelled by manifest necessity or infirmity." Exceptions to this requirement were made frequently, for reasons of time, expediency, and safety, but Serra was determined to walk to Mexico City. (This trek has given rise to what Serra's biographer Father Maynard Geiger has called the "unconquerable legend" that the priest always walked in carrying out his missions of conversion and exploration

A view of Veracruz, Mexico, where Serra landed in December 1749. Although the Crown provided horses to transport the priests to Mexico City, Serra insisted on walking the 200 miles. This feat gave rise to the legend, rejected by historians, that all his travels in the New World were made on foot.

in the New World. In fact, it is clear from documentary evidence that on most of his journeys in Mexico and California, Serra did not walk. The distances he had to travel were simply too great, the demands on his time too heavy, and his own responsibilities too numerous to allow him to do so.)

Wayfarers traveled from Veracruz to Mexico City along the Camino Real, or King's Highway, but this impressive title was highly misleading. The Camino Real was little more than a crude dirt road, often impassable in bad weather, on which travelers were menaced by Indians, rockslides, bandits, and wild animals. Still, it connected some of New Spain's most distant outposts. With Mexico City as its hub, it stretched 200 miles east to Veracruz on the Atlantic Ocean, another 200 miles southwest to Acapulco on the Pacific, and more than 1,000 miles north-south from Santa Fe (the present-day capital of New Mexico) to the jungles of Central America.

It took Serra and his only companion, a Franciscan from the Spanish region of Andalusia whose name has been lost to history, about 18 days to reach Mexico City. Their journey took them from the lush coast, with its overabundance of tropical growth, into and across the Sierra Madre Oriental, the rugged mountain range that separates Mexico's Atlantic coast from its central plateau, where the bulk of the population, then as now, made its home. (In earlier times, the Atlantic coast had been much more heavily populated, but the epidemics introduced by the Spanish newcomers did some of their most devastating work there.) The two priests carried no provisions, preferring instead, as true mendicants, to beg for their food and shelter from the local people "for the love of God." On many nights, the priests simply slept in the open, using a bed of moss or the hard ground as their pillow. Serra, as was his lifelong habit, slept on his back, his cross clutched firmly in his hands and resting on his chest. Although the region of Mexico they traveled through is generally warm, the nights could get quite chilly, and on at least one occasion the priests awoke to find frost on the ground and the streams frozen.

They set out each day shortly after sunrise, immediately following the morning mass. Quickly the sun climbed higher, and by noon on most days the coarse gray robes of the travelers would be damp and heavy with sweat. Along the coast, parrots and other tropical birds screamed raucously, but the way grew quieter as the pair climbed into the mountains. There, the snow lay year-round on the peaks and along the ridges of the frosty canyons; the cry of wolves echoed at night along the lonely valleys; and mountain lions prowled their solitary domains. It was not unheard of for bandits to swoop down on unprotected travelers in these mountains, but Serra, as ever, put his trust in God and remained unconcerned.

Mexico City as it appeared after the Aztec buildings had been destroyed and replaced with Spanish-style architecture. When Serra arrived there in 1750, the capital's wealthy families were eager to entertain him, but he was interested only in pursuing his work as a missionary.

According to the account of his journey that Serra later rendered to Palóu, the two friars were rewarded several times over for their faith. On one occasion, as night descended, the priests found themselves stranded in a particularly desolate region on the banks of a raging river, with no way to cross to the other side, where they had hoped to reach shelter in a small village. Despairingly, Serra cried out, only to be answered by the voice of a man who had suddenly materialized in the dusk on the river's far shore. This mysterious stranger indicated that the priests should walk downstream, where they would find a shallow place to ford the river. They did so, and the man met them on the opposite bank. He took them to his home, fed them, and offered them shelter for the night, but he remained reticent and evasive in conversation. The next day, when the priests awoke, they discovered that overnight the temperature had plummeted, and snow and ice covered the ground. Serra had no doubt that he and his companion would have frozen to death had it not been for the timely intercession of their well-dressed and courteous benefactor, whose name they had not even been able to learn.

Some days later, the wayfarers paused for a rest at the end of another long, arduous day of travel. They were exhausted and famished, for "the table of the Lord" had been bare for several days. A horse and rider suddenly appeared on the horizon, cantering in the opposite direction from the one in which the friars were traveling. The horseman drew to a stop near the tired padres and offered each a single pomegranate. Then he rode on, leaving the two to speculate on his resemblance to their mysterious rescuer of several days past. They thankfully devoured the tart, pulpy berry, which they found restorative and nourishing out of all proportion to its size. Feeling remarkably rejuvenated, they were able to continue their journey.

A couple of days farther along the Camino Real, the two priests stayed overnight on a small farm, whose owner had allowed them to bed down on some straw in the stable. In the morning, after

Serra celebrated the Mass, the farmer gave them a loaf of bread to sustain them on their way. Later that day, they encountered a beggar. The priests gave the ragged, emaciated man their loaf, the only food they had. That evening, as they lay collapsed and weary on the side of the road, the horseman and his mount appeared again. The rider removed a small, misshapen loaf of bread from his saddlebag, cut it in two with his dagger, and gave half to each priest. The bread was so lumpy and foul smelling that at first Serra and his friend were afraid to eat it, but eventually hunger got the best of them. Again, they found the unexpected repast, so meager in portion, to be incredibly delicious and revivifying. Serra concluded that the mystifying provider was none other than St. Joseph, the stepfather of Christ, transformed into a New World hidalgo.

St. Joseph may have been able to scare off the wolf of starvation, but he proved to be no match for a much smaller adversary—the *zancudo,* a fierce Mexican mosquito. These nasty little bugs were a scourge to travelers on the Camino Real, and swarms of them regularly tormented the two frailes andariegos; their bites could cause illness and even death under certain circumstances. Near the conclusion of his journey, Serra noticed a maddening itch and some swelling on his left foot. In his customary fashion, he ignored the discomfort and trudged on, but his foot grew grotesquely swollen and enormously painful. By nightfall, he could not walk; by daybreak, he was feverish and delirious, and the infection had spread well up his left leg. After a couple of days' rest, he was able to continue, but only through sheer strength of will. He attributed the infection to a bite from a zancudo. But modern scholars have suggested that the problem stemmed from a brown recluse spider (sometimes called the fiddler spider), whose bite is initially painless but leaves a highly toxic venom that over time causes gangrenous ulceration of the skin. Whatever the cause of his affliction, when Serra limped into Mexico City and through the gates of the Apostolic College of San Fernando on New Year's Day, 1750, a massive open sore covered much of the lower part of his left leg and a good portion of his left foot. Nevertheless, he steadfastly refused medical treatment whenever it was proffered. The leg was to pain him for the rest of his days, with only occasional periods of relief.

It was traditional for would-be missionaries to spend a year at the College of San Fernando in cloistered seclusion before being sent into the wilderness. During that time, they were to prepare themselves spiritually, mentally, and physically for the daunting challenges ahead of them. They took classes in the languages of the Indian tribes to whom they would be sent, occasionally spoke with more experienced missionaries, and received instruction in some of the practical things they would need to know, such as agriculture. Serra adapted quickly to this routine and also earned a reputation for the brilliance of his sermons, to the extent that some of the friars petitioned the guardian, or head of the college, Joseph Ortís de Velasco, to refrain from sending him to a mission posting. Such eloquence would be wasted on the illiterate, heathen Indians, they reasoned; Serra could be of much greater service in Mexico City, preaching to its faithful, whose souls were in constant peril from all the temptations that a prosperous capital city could offer. Serra, however, would have none of it. Long before the year was over for Serra's contingent of prospective missionaries, Father Velasco told them that the missions in the Sierra Gorda were in such desperate need of priests that he was forced to request several volunteers to go there immediately. Serra replied instantly, echoing the words used in the Old Testament by the prophet Isaiah when commending himself as an instrument of God's will: "Here I am, send me." He and eight others were chosen to fill vacancies in the Sierra Gorda. Velasco asked Serra to become the president of the five missions located there, but this time he declined, stating that he preferred to begin his work as a simple missionary. The simple missionary was to become one of the most important figures in the history of New Spain.

An 16th-century painting shows Father Serra supervising the erection of a cross. Serra performed the Stations of the Cross at the mission in Jalpan as a means of impressing the Indians with the drama and pagentry of the Catholic ritual.

CHAPTER FIVE

The Mother of the Sun

The Sierra Gorda region lies about 200 miles north-northeast of Mexico City, in the approximate middle of the Sierra Madre Oriental. The town where Serra was to be posted, Jalpan, is in the present-day Mexican state of Querétaro. At the time of his arrival there on June 16, 1750, it was a dusty collection of primitive adobe dwellings with thatched roofs, nestled at the base of an 11,000-foot mountain. Even the church was little more than a jacal, or adobe hut. A quick reconnaissance of the other four mission towns in the region—Landa, Concá, Tancoyol, and Tilaco—revealed to Serra that they were in no better shape.

The Pame Indians, the original inhabitants of the region, had long been among the most implacable opponents of the Spanish. They harassed settlers, ambushed soldiers, and steadfastly resisted the attempts made by missionaries to "reduce" them. (*Reducción* was the Spanish term for the process of persuading—or coercing—the Indians to abandon their native way of existence, embrace Christianity, and live as peasant laborers.) Some inroads were made in the 1740s by Colonel José de Escandón and Father Mezquía. The

61

former defeated the Pame in battle; the latter convinced them to listen to the missionaries he intended to send to the region. Mezquía dispatched 8 friars from the College of San Fernando, and over the period of a few years 7,000 Indians came into the missions. The Indians were motivated in some cases by the compassion and concern shown them by the missionaries but more often by the destruction of their villages by Spanish soldiers. The process of reduction in the Sierra Gorda was successful at first, but epidemics, probably of smallpox, killed two-thirds of the mission Indians, and the others soon returned to the mountains. Four of the priests themselves fell victim to disease, and the remaining four returned in discouragement to Mexico City.

Serra had been told he would find 1,000 active parishioners at Jalpan, but he soon discovered that this figure had been greatly exaggerated by his predecessors. In fact, of the Indians who maintained some contact with the scraggly village, not one attended mass or received confession even once a year. These Indians certainly were reduced. They were starving, uprooted, greatly diminished in numbers, and much abused by the Spanish soldiers who manned the presidio, or fortress, that served as a garrison for the missions—but they could not really be called Christians. Serra had a plan to change that.

He began by implementing the rules Mezquía had first developed during his time as a missionary in Texas. At sunrise, the mission bell rang, issuing a clangorous summons for all the Indians in the area to assemble at the church. Attendance was mandatory and was sometimes enforced by the soldiers. One of the priests—sometimes Serra, who had taken lessons in the Pame language, sometimes Palóu, who had also been posted to Jalpan—said prayers and gave a lesson on their meaning. The prayers were said in Latin, and Serra or Palóu then explained them either in the Pame tongue or in Spanish, in which case an Indian interpreter translated. Special instructional classes were given twice daily for children above the age of five. On Sundays and feast days, all

Indians were required to attend mass. At the conclusion of the service, they were made to file by one at a time to kiss the priest's hand, at which time attendance was taken. Those who skipped mass might be rounded up and persuaded—through earnest entreaty, a whipping, or imprisonment—to renounce their pagan ways. Attendance at funerals was also mandatory. Obviously, the Indians were forbidden to engage in witchcraft, devil worship, or idolatry, as the Spanish alternately termed the practice of the Indians' native religion.

Although Serra was the instrument of a system that was inherently brutal and coercive to the inhabitants of the New World, he preferred, because of his personality, intellect, and conscience, to convert through gentle persuasion rather than force. He might use soldiers to round up recalcitrant Indians and bring them into the missions, but he was forceful in his denunciation of the rapes that Spanish soldiers habitually committed on Indian women. He also opposed the efforts of the military to encroach on mission land, which was intended for use by the Indians to grow pumpkins, corn, beans, and other produce for subsistence and for sale in the market. Indian revelers at "pagan" dances (which were in actuality native religious ceremonies, performed to ensure good fortune, a bountiful harvest, happiness in marriage, the safety of a child, and so on) might be whipped, but Serra realized that fear alone would not be sufficient to stamp out the Indian religion.

Atop a peak in the Sierra Gorda stood an Indian temple dedicated to the divinity Cachum, whom the Pame revered as the mother of the sun and whose likeness, carved in exquisite marble, reposed there. A long stone stairway, along which the Indians buried their chiefs and other prominent individuals, led to the temple and the statue. Much like the peasants of Petra, who climbed to the hillside shrine of Nuestra Señora de Bon Any to leave offerings, make penance, and seek good fortune, the Indians of the Sierra Gorda ascended to this mountainside temple to pray in their own fashion.

64

An 18th-century Spanish map of the Sierra Gorda region of Mexico shows the settlements to which Junípero Serra was assigned as a missionary in 1750. Upon arriving in the area, Serra found that the missions were extremely primitive; even the churches were often nothing more than adobe huts.

Contemplating these rituals, Serra realized that it would be possible to reach the Pame Indians with the message of Christianity in the same way that the Catholic church reached the peasants of Majorca. Rather than order the soldiers to tear down Cachum's shrine—missionaries elsewhere in New Spain frequently destroyed native religious buildings and artifacts—Serra decided to appeal to the natives with the same sense of drama and pageantry that was common to both his religion and theirs. Although he had no training in engineering or architecture, he drew up plans for the construction of a large cross and 14 elaborate stations on a hillside near the church in Jalpan.

In Catholic ceremony, the Stations of the Cross represent the various events that befell Christ on his way to crucifixion on Calvary—his being jeered by the crowd, his stumbling under the weight of the cross, his donning the crown of thorns. By making the Stations of the Cross—that is, by engaging in prayers and ritual acts of atonement and remembrance at each of the 14 designated stations—Catholics symbolically participate in Christ's passion, death, and (by extension) resurrection. The Stations of the Cross are usually performed during Holy Week (the 7 days culminating in Easter Sunday) and Lent (the 40 days before Easter, a period of symbolic renunciation and abstinence). At the time Serra was doing his work in the Sierra Gorda, the Stations of the Cross were still a relatively new innovation in Catholic observances and were reserved exclusively for the Franciscans, by order of the pope.

Serra ordered the stations built in ascending order on the hillside leading up to the cross, hoping thereby to provide a substitute for the sacred stairway leading to the temple of Cachum. On Good Friday, 1751, the Stations of the Cross were made in Jalpan for the first time. Serra himself shouldered a heavy wooden cross hewn from a nearby forest and carried it up the hillside in a symbolic reenactment of Christ's ordeal. At the summit, a wooden Christ figure made by Serra was nailed to the timber, while Serra chanted prayers and the soldiers fired their rifles into the air. Then the effigy—which had movable arms and legs—was taken down from the cross and laid in a coffin. Two days later, on Easter Sunday, the feast day on which Catholics celebrate the Resurrection, the Christ figure was removed from the coffin and paraded around Jalpan in a triumphal procession.

Other feast days during the year were celebrated with similar pomp. Each Sunday night, a torchlight parade was held in honor of the Virgin Mary, and Serra even wrote and arranged the performances of several mystery plays, simple dramas intended to illustrate essential tenets of Catholic belief. The pageantry was so effective that Spaniards came from many miles away to attend the services.

What the Indians thought is harder to say, for they left no written records behind them. Although Palóu reports that he and Serra won many converts, and this is undoubtedly true, it is impossible to judge the motivation of the Indians. For many of them, with their homes destroyed and their crops burned, the choice was

The Pame Indians, the native inhabitants of the Sierra Gorda, were known for their resistance to Spanish rule. "The truth is," Serra later wrote, "I have always found these poor pagans very lovable." He often used his authority to protect the Indians from being abused by the soldiers.

between conversion and starvation. Simple demoralization no doubt also played a decisive role; with so many of their family, friends, and compatriots dead or converted, many of the Pame simply lost the will to resist. In any event, Serra somehow came into possession of the likeness of Cachum. Supposedly, the Indian entrusted with guarding it presented it to him as a symbol of the Pame conversion to Catholicism. On a visit to Mexico City in late 1752, Serra presented the image to the guardian of the College of San Fernando as tangible evidence of the progress he was making at Jalpan. He asked, according to Palóu, "that it be put in the box of archives belonging to the documents and papers of these Missions as a memento of the Spiritual conquest."

Serra returned from his Mexico City trip as the president of all five of the Sierra Gorda missions. He now had another enterprise in mind—the construction of a new stone church at Jalpan to replace the crude adobe structure that had been serving as a house of worship. Serra himself drew up the plans and took part in the construction, carrying beams and shoring up the walls, although he had brought with him from the capital several trained carpenters, masons, and blacksmiths to oversee and perform the most difficult work. The bulk of the building was done in the cooler, dry seasons between the end of October and April, when the Indians were free from their work in the fields and available to

This drawing of Serra's San Carlos mission shows the typical architecture of the early settlements. When Serra became president of the Sierra Gorda missions, his first project was to build a new church at Jalpan. Visitors were often surprised to see him carrying beams and stones alongside the hired laborers.

serve as common laborers. Several of the Pame served a sort of apprenticeship to the skilled artisans. All told, the Church of Santiago de Jalpan, with its 90-foot bell tower, took 7 years to complete.

When not working on the church, Serra concerned himself with the ongoing process of reducing the Pame. He brought with him from Mexico City oxen, goats, sheep, and donkeys, which he distributed to the more ambitious farmers among the Pame. According to Palóu's account, the Indians soon became such ardent agriculturalists that they were able to sell their excess food to other towns. When his duties at Jalpan permitted, Serra visited the other missions of the Sierra Gorda in his new capacity as president for the region. At his instigation, the Franciscans at each of these towns soon began construction work on churches of their own.

Serra also had new responsibilities as the inquisitor general for the region. He was charged, as the agent of the dreaded Spanish Inquisition, with rooting out heresy. Serra himself had asked that an agent be appointed for the region because of an alarming rise in incidents of "witchcraft" and "devil worship," not on the part of the Indians but by Spanish settlers in the region. Serra reported back to the Holy Office that a Mexican woman named Cayetana had testified to evil practices by the *gente de razón* (people of reason), a term the Spaniards used to differentiate themselves from the "superstitious" Indians. According to Cayetana, a number of individuals "flying through the air at night are in the habit of meeting in a cave on a hill near a ranch called El Saucillo, . . . where they worship and make sacrifice to the demons who appear visibly there in the guise of young goats and various other things of that nature."

Whether Serra actually put any stock in these charges is uncertain. He would more likely have concerned himself with the adoption of Indian customs by Spaniards, a trend that recent historians have found to be more widespread than was previously believed. In many cases, young European men were attracted by the sexual freedom practiced by the Indians; the allure was especially strong in areas where there were not enough marriageable women and where religious and social constraints on sexual relations outside of marriage were strong. (Most Indian cultures had a more tolerant notion of the bounds of acceptable sexual conduct than did European or colonial societies at the time.) The Inquisition's agents were empowered to punish offenders by burning them at the stake, although there is no record of Serra utilizing this power. What steps he did take to deal with the problem remain unknown.

As always during his life, Serra amazed all those who knew him with his seemingly inexhaustible energy. His days passed quickly, in a welter of duties and tasks—the daily prayers, mass, and religious instruction; the work on the church; tending to the sick in the mission infirmary; administering the sacraments; keeping the Apostolic College informed of the progress of the missions in the Sierra Gorda. Finally, in September 1758, Serra received a summons from Mexico City. Two missionaries had been killed in Texas, where they had been laboring unsuccessfully to reduce the unyielding Apache; Serra and Palóu were needed to take their place. As soon as Serra received this news, Palóu wrote, his face became "radiant with a new joy and happiness," and he immediately "left the Mission in which he had labored for nearly nine years." The work that was to be his most enduring legacy was about to begin.

A Comanche chief, as drawn by the American artist George Catlin. In 1758, the Comanche attacked and destroyed the Spanish mission on the San Saba River in Texas. The following year, Junípero Serra was sent to San Saba to replace the missionaries who had been slain in the assault.

CHAPTER SIX

Penance and Solitude

Alonso Giraldo Terreros and José Santiestevan, the two friars whose death had necessitated Serra and Palóu's return to Mexico City, had been serving in Texas at a mission on the San Saba River. The mission had been founded with money provided by Terreros's cousin, Pedro Romero de Terreros, who had made a fortune in the Mexican silver mines. The Spanish had held high hopes for the mission's success because the request for its foundation had been made to the Spanish authorities by a delegation of Apache Indians at the recently founded settlement of San Antonio. Prior to the arrival of this delegation, the Apache had ferociously opposed all Spanish encroachments onto the Texas plains, so the Spanish were naturally encouraged by this change of heart. What they did not realize—prejudiced as they were by their notion of the Indians as unsophisticated savages—was that the Apache were preparing an act of deception worthy of the most devious intriguer from any European embassy. In the best style of European diplomacy, the Apache were attempting to play off against each other their two

most hated enemies, the Spanish and the Comanche. The Comanche, armed with rifles obtained from French traders and riding
horses either bought or stolen from the Spanish, were the most
powerful Indian tribe on the Great Plains. The Apache hoped that
the Spanish would act on their offer and establish a mission, which
the Comanche, no more desirous than the Apache of having the
Spanish in their territory, would then destroy. The result, according
to the Apache's plan, would be mutually destructive warfare between the Spanish and the Comanche, leaving the Apache as the
strongest power in the region.

Three brave friars—Terreros, Santiestevan, and Miguel Molina—established the mission of San Saba de la Santa Cruz in April
1757. But to their eternal disappointment, they were unable to
persuade a single Apache to convert or to resettle on mission land.
Occasionally, groups of Apache would wander in to accept the
gifts—food, bolts of cloth, glass beads, and other trinkets—that the
priests distributed in an attempt to initiate relations, but then the
Indians would mock and jeer the padres, spit at them, and taunt
them. Ultimately, the Franciscans got the message. They sent
several letters confessing their failure to the Apostolic College and
even to the viceroy of New Spain, but each time they were instructed to stay where they were and continue their efforts.

On the morning of March 16, 1758, 2,000 Indian warriors,
most of them Comanche, some of them Wichita, swooped down on
the defenseless mission. The Indians were mounted on horseback
and armed with rifles; at least one of their chiefs was wearing a
French military uniform. (Because France's claims in the New
World abutted and even overlapped those of its frequent enemy,
Spain, the French sometimes made use of the Indians to harass the
Spanish.) Terreros and Santiestevan were quickly killed, the latter
while he knelt at the altar in the mission church in desperate
prayer; he was then beheaded. Molina was badly wounded, but he
managed to hide and then somehow make it back to safety. After
their work at the mission was done, the Indians galloped two miles

upriver and easily routed the small Spanish garrison at the presidio of San Luis de las Amarillas.

Serra arrived in Mexico City from the Sierra Gorda on September 26, 1759. At the Apostolic College of San Fernando, he heard the tale of the massacre from the still-recuperating Father Molina, an old friend who had come to the New World with him aboard the *Villasota*. The seeming hopelessness of restoring the San Saba mission only fired Serra's zeal for the task. "I realize my feebleness and nothingness for so glorious an enterprise," he wrote to his nephew, Miguel de Petra, who had recently been ordained as a Capuchin priest back on Majorca.

While Serra was eagerly preparing to depart, the Spanish at San Antonio were organizing a massive punitive expedition to smash the Comanche. Consisting of 600 soldiers, 2 huge cannons, and a long supply train, it was comparable in size to the force Cortés had used to conquer all of Mexico, but it met with less success. On October 7, the Spanish troops encountered a force of several thousand Comanche, Wichita, and other Plains Indians entrenched behind well-engineered defensive breastworks along the Red River. The Spanish attempted to mount a siege, but after four hours they were thoroughly routed. It was one of the most decisive military defeats the Spanish ever received in the New World and essentially halted Spain's efforts to expand its influence in Texas.

The mission at San Saba was never reestablished. Serra and Palóu were both still eager to go, despite this newest evidence of Indian intransigence. But Pedro Romero de Terreros, the mission's financial backer, insisted on his continued right to name the missionaries who would serve there. The standoff between him and the Apostolic College, which insisted on Serra and Palóu, combined with the unlikely prospect of reducing the Comanche or the Apache, resulted in the project's abandonment.

Serra did not return to the Sierra Gorda but remained instead at the Apostolic College, where he served for the next nine years as choirmaster and supervisor of novices. Although Serra enjoyed

A 19th-century drawing shows a group of men and women expressing their religious fervor by practicing flagellation. While preaching in Mexico City, Serra would often call himself a sinner and lash himself unmercifully until the parishioners begged him to stop.

company and always made loyal friends wherever he went, he apparently took no part in the social life of Mexico City, where priests were often invited into the most fashionable homes and were frequently adopted as spiritual advisers by the leading families. Indeed, it was a mark of distinction for a family to number one of the city's renowned clerics among its social set, but according to Palóu "there was no person in the city whom he [Serra] would ever visit." Those who wished to avail themselves of Serra's spiritual counsel, as adviser or confessor, had to come to the college to see him. Many people did so because Serra's reputation for learning, eloquence, and devotion had preceded him from the Sierra Gorda and had only been enhanced by the fiery sermons he roused himself to deliver.

During this time, Serra's devotion to self-denial reached new heights. He regularly engaged in rituals of mortification of the flesh, intended to purge the body of its demands and consequently strengthen the spirit. He rarely slept, fasted often, and regularly kept nightlong prayer vigils. In the middle of the night, when he believed no one would notice, he crept into the choir loft and vigorously whipped his naked body, tearing huge strips from his skin. He wove spiky strands of wire into his gray friar's robe, facing inward so that they constantly raked his flesh. Sometimes he intensified this sartorial torture by donning a sackcloth of rough bristles, which scratched and tore at his already damaged skin. He made frequent journeys to rural parishes in remote regions surrounding Mexico City, such as Puebla, Valladolid, and Oaxaca, often as a fraile andariego, and preached lengthy, impassioned sermons. On more than one occasion, while attempting to impress upon his congregation that all men, even the most seemingly exalted, were nothing more than pitiful sinners and desperately needed to repent, he dropped his robe to his waist and began beating his chest with a large stone and his ever-present crucifix. The parishioners would plead with him to stop for fear that he would crush his own chest cavity. At other times, while preaching, he would hold his hand in the flame of a candle until his flesh bubbled and blistered. In the course of perhaps his most memorable sermon, he dropped his robe to his waist, exposing his frail upper torso, and lashed himself so fiercely with a heavy chain that most of the audience began sobbing. Overcome with a sense of his own unworthiness, a man from the congregation rushed up onto the altar, stripped to the waist, seized the chain from Serra, and energetically performed his own public penance. He beat himself unrelentingly, calling out, "I am the ungrateful sinner before God who should do penance and not the Father, who is a saint," and collapsed. Serra then gave him both Holy Communion and the last rites; the man died a short time later.

Such practices were intended to bring Serra closer to God by weakening the flesh, whose desires were seen as being the root of most sin. Whether they had the intended effect must remain a mystery, for according to Palóu, Serra never spoke of his inner life. And although Serra always obeyed uncomplainingly the dictates of his order, the nine years he spent at San Fernando must have been frustrating ones, for he had not changed his belief that one could best serve God as a missionary. As he once expressed his feelings to Palóu, "I have had no other motive but to revive in my soul those intense longings which I have had since my novitiate when I read the lives of the saints." Perhaps Serra's ritual self-mortification was his reaction to being denied an opportunity to do the work that he felt brought him closest to Christ, so he utilized another extreme way to approach his savior.

In the summer of 1767, a new opportunity for Serra to exercise his calling as a missionary presented itself. In June of that year, Spanish officials in Mexico enacted the first of several edicts issued by King Charles III that would eventually result in the expulsion of the Jesuits (the members of the religious order the Society of Jesus) from all Spanish territory in the New World and ultimately from Spain itself.

The expulsion was an absolutely stunning and unforeseen development, for the Society of Jesus had been founded by a Spanish monk, St. Ignatius of Loyola, in 1540. The Jesuits were renowned for their missionary and educational work, which had taken them to every inhabited continent of the globe except for Australia. But the success of the order was in some ways its downfall. The Jesuits earned a reputation for learning and teaching but also for secretiveness, greed, and a certain deviousness. The order grew immensely powerful and wealthy, but its insistence on independence in conducting its affairs made a number of monarchs and even the pope suspicious. The Jesuit missionaries in South America, for

St. Ignatius of Loyola (1491–1556), as portrayed in a 17th-century painting by Peter Paul Rubens. Loyola founded the Society of Jesus in 1540, and the society's members, the Jesuits, distinguished themselves as teachers and missionaries. However, their growing power resulted in their expulsion from the New World.

example, who consistently opposed attempts to enslave or otherwise exploit the Indians, were accused of plotting to establish separate Jesuit states there. The breaking point came when Charles III was shown a forged letter supposedly written by the superior general of the Society of Jesus. The alleged author claimed to have evidence, to be publicized at the right moment, that the king had been born illegitimately. If proved correct, such a charge could threaten the king's right to his throne.

On the morning of June 25, 1767, in a carefully coordinated operation, soldiers surrounded all of the 29 Jesuit missions and houses of worship in Mexico. The king's decree of expulsion was read to the bewildered missionaries, and the soldiers seized all their property along with the missions. The priests were given no time to

pack their belongings; with only their prayer books and the garments they were wearing, they were taken into custody and hustled off to Veracruz. Those that survived the torturous journey—many did not—were to be shipped back to Spain. The king's decree required that all Jesuits in Mexico be transported as prisoners to Veracruz within 24 hours. "If after the embarkation there should be found one Jesuit in that district, even if ill or dying," the decree stated, the government officials responsible for implementing the order would "suffer the penalty of death."

At the time of the expulsion, Serra was sermonizing in the peaceful Indian village of Ixmiquilpan. He received an urgent summons to return to Mexico City, where the guardian of the Apostolic College of San Fernando, José García, explained that Serra was being assigned to a new position. The now gray-haired and middle-aged Junípero Serra was to be president of the former Jesuit missions, which were to be run by the Franciscans, on the long, desolate peninsula known as Baja California. Not many people would have welcomed such an assignment. Baja California was an arid, cactus-choked region called by the unfortunate Spanish soldiers who were posted there *el último rincón del mundo*— the last corner of the earth.

The Indians of Baja California struggled to survive in the arid conditions of their homeland. Unable to grow crops, they lived a nomadic existence; seafood and desert plants made up much of their diet, and the skins of deer and birds served them as clothing.

CHAPTER SEVEN

California

Baja California, 800 miles long and varying in width from 35 to 145 miles, extends southward into the Pacific Ocean from the present-day border between Mexico and the state of California. The Gulf of California separates it from the Mexican mainland. Mountains run virtually its entire length, but the central region is mainly desert. Except for its southern tip, where tropical vegetation grows, Baja California has an extremely dry climate, and its soil and water are both notable for their exceptional alkaline content, making agriculture extremely difficult. One type of plant is perfectly suited to the environment, however; more varieties of cactus grow on the peninsula than anywhere else in the world. As Father Juan Crespí described it, Baja California was "sterile, arid, lacking grass and water, and abounding in stones and thorns."

Cortés was responsible for the Spanish presence in the Baja. In 1533, he dispatched a ship from Tehuantepec across the Gulf of California to explore the peninsula's northern regions, but the crew mutinied and murdered its captain; shortly after landing at La

Paz, most of them were in turn massacred by the Indians. Cortés himself came to the peninsula in 1535 and established a small colony at La Paz, which he renamed Santa Cruz, but the settlement lasted less than a year. During that time, pearls were found in the waters of the Gulf of California. This discovery briefly whetted Spain's interest in the peninsula, but subsequent colonization efforts failed, mainly because the climate and soil defeated attempts to establish agriculture and it was too difficult to supply outposts from across the gulf. Explorers occasionally visited the remote region, most notably Sebastián Vizcaíno in 1596, but the first permanent Spanish settlement in Baja California was not established until 1697. That year, at Loreto, the missionary Juan María Salvatierra founded the first of 21 Jesuit missions on the peninsula.

Although the Spanish found Baja California forbidding and desolate, it supported a large number of Indian tribes. The Jesuits estimated that there were 40,000 Indians living on the peninsula when they arrived. The missionaries (and many succeeding commentators) reported that the Baja Indians were unusually primitive, ill clad when not altogether naked, and given to a nomadic way of life that left them constantly on the verge of starvation. But the Indians had in fact developed a number of methods that allowed them to exist in harmony with their environment. It was the Spanish newcomers to the peninsula who were most often in danger of starvation, particularly when supply ships did not arrive as scheduled. Many of the missionaries, including Serra, described the Baja Indians as a handsome, physically attractive people. This contradicted the portrayal of them as famished wretches badly in need of the civilizing influences of the missions, a frequently stated justification for the Spanish presence in the region.

The Spanish missions on the Baja were among the most successful in the history of New Spain when it came to the business of reduction. By the spring of 1768, when Serra and his team of 15 Franciscan missionaries landed at Loreto aboard *La Purísima Concepción de María Santísima* (the Immaculate Conception of Holy

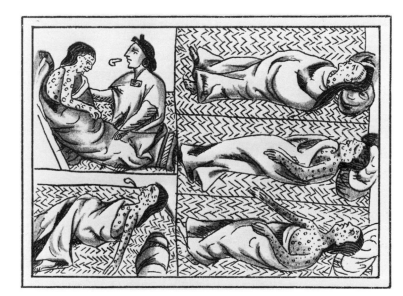

This drawing from an Aztec manuscript illustrates the fatal progress of smallpox. As in Mexico, European diseases spread rapidly among the Baja Indians. They died in such numbers that it was difficult for the missionaries to establish large and stable settlements.

Mary), their census revealed that the Indian population on the peninsula had diminished by more than 80 percent, to just 7,000 people. In bringing the Indians into the missions, the Jesuits and the soldiers had relied on force as well as moral persuasion. The Indians were driven away from their own lands and sometimes transferred en masse to distant regions of the peninsula, where they were made to mingle with unfamiliar Indians from other tribes.

The cultural shock inherent in these events was enough to disrupt and slow Indian birth rates, while the displacement of various populations encouraged the spread of European diseases from one Indian people to another. Some missions recorded 1,000 deaths annually. Smallpox and syphilis seem to have been the primary culprits, but tuberculosis, typhus, measles, and malaria also wreaked havoc. During the year that Serra spent in the Baja, an epidemic of smallpox, followed by a deadly outbreak of measles, killed off 15 percent of the Indian population. By that point, the infant mortality rate among the Baja Indians was approaching 100 percent. Disease no doubt killed the majority, but it is also possible

that the Indians had become so demoralized that women decided
to abort or kill their children rather than allow them to live such a
miserable existence. (Such practices were verified in later years
among Indian tribes elsewhere in California.) Palóu noted ac-
curately that "if it goes on at this rate, in a short time Baja California
will come to an end."

Serra spent barely more than a year in Baja California, most of
it at Loreto, a depressing outpost near the Gulf of California.
Although it served in name and function as the capital of the Baja
region, Loreto was little more than a collection of small mud huts,
which housed both Indians and soldiers, although not together.
There was no running water. The mission itself was a rectangular
adobe structure with a flat roof; it served as both a dwelling place
for Serra and the governor, Gaspar de Portolá, and a storeroom for
beef, tallow, lard, cloth, sugar, chocolate, wheat, leather, and corn,
almost all of it brought across the gulf. Portolá had been charged
with the grim task of expelling the Jesuits. At the time of Serra's
arrival on the peninsula, some of these unfortunates were still
being held in hastily erected, rat-infested, straw-and-mud barracks
at the coastal settlement of Guaymas. They were given inadequate
food and water, and many succumbed to a variety of illnesses.

To his dismay, Serra soon learned that the missionaries in Baja
California were to assume responsibility for only spiritual affairs.
Control over supplies, land, even the church buildings themselves
were to remain in the hands of the soldiers who had been occupy-
ing the various missions since the expulsion of the Jesuits. Serra
argued, to no avail, that such a system was unworkable; in order to
succeed, he pleaded, the priests needed total administrative control of each individual mission, as had always previously been the
case in Mexico.

Upon arriving at their respective assignments, Serra's missionaries recognized the truth of their president's argument. The
mission at Loreto had been grim and ramshackle, but it was by far
the most elegant on the peninsula. The remainder were in a truly

José Gálvez (1729–87) was appointed inspector general in 1768 and given power to reform the colonial government of Mexico. Finding the Mexican missions in a run-down condition, he transferred control of them from the soldiers to Serra's missionaries.

appalling state of disrepair. Worse, most of the Indians had run off because of the excesses of the soldiers, who had not bothered to bring them back. Instead, obsessed with rumors of the hoards of gold the Jesuits were supposed to have secreted, the soldiers had plundered and ransacked the mission stores. Cattle were slaughtered by the hundreds, crops were ruined, and many months' worth of supplies were stolen. After making a tour of inspection in the summer of 1768, José Gálvez, the recently appointed inspector general, was so disturbed by the waste that he ordered that control of the missions be returned immediately to Serra's missionaries. (As inspector general, Gálvez had been given extraordinary power by the king to effect changes in Spain's colonial government in Mexico. His powers exceeded even those of the viceroy, who was normally the highest-ranking government official in the New World.)

The new policy did not appreciably better the lot of the Indians, however, and the missions were in such a state of disarray that not even Serra's prodigious energy was sufficient to rejuvenate them in the short time he was there. Gálvez continued to insist on shifting various Indian populations to new locations, and the Indians continued to sicken and die. Only Father Fermín Lasuén, at the remote Mission San Borja, objected to this practice. Despite Gálvez's insistence, Lasuén consistently frustrated the inspector general's attempts to relocate the San Borja Indians.

Perhaps one reason for Serra's relative lack of success in the Baja was that almost as soon as he arrived there, he began readying himself for a new challenge: Gálvez, who had taken the indomitable padre into his confidence, was planning a colonizing expedition to the region the Spanish called Alta California. (In Spanish, *alta* means "high," and *baja* means "low"; hence, Upper and Lower California. Alta California was essentially the region that is today the state of California.)

Spain based its claims to Alta California on the voyages of exploration carried out in 1542 by João Rodrigues Cabrilho, a Portuguese-born explorer then in the service of the Spanish crown. Cabrilho had served with Cortés in the conquest of Mexico; in 1542 he explored the length of the California coast, discovering, among other things, beautiful natural harbors at what would later become San Diego and Monterey, California. It would be 60 years before another Spanish mariner, Sebastián Vizcaíno, returned to California. Vizcaíno reiterated Cabrilho's praise for San Diego and Monterey harbors and anchored his ship at Point Reyes, just north of what would later be San Francisco, California. In the meantime, in 1579, California's coast was visited by an English explorer, Sir Francis Drake, who was characterized as "the master thief of the unknown world" by the scornful Spanish, whose gold- and silver-laden galleons he regularly plundered. Drake also anchored near the San Francisco Bay, which he understatedly described as a "conveynient harborough." He then claimed California—he called it New Albion, using an ancient name for Britain—on behalf of his monarch, Queen Elizabeth I.

For more than 160 years after Vizcaíno's expedition, Spain did not act upon its claim to Alta California, primarily because it devoted its energies and moneys to exploring, pacifying, settling, and administering its other New World dominions. When Spain renewed its interest in the region at the end of the 1760s, it was not because the Crown suddenly had new resources to spare or believed that colonization would be immediately profitable. The idea was rather to stave off competition: Russia had established settlements on the west coast of North America, from Alaska almost as far southward as Point Reyes, and England was also exhibiting a renewed interest in the land that Drake had claimed. Although Spain was unprepared at that time to make a major commitment to settling California, it did not wish the territory to fall into the hands of these rivals.

Because Spain had neither money nor manpower to spare, Gálvez's plan for the settlement of California relied on the intrepid Franciscan missionaries, particularly Junípero Serra, for its success.

A 19th-century engraving shows Sir Francis Drake, the English pirate and explorer, being greeted by California Indians. Drake weighed anchor near the site of present-day San Francisco and claimed California for the English crown. Competition from England and Russia spurred the Spanish to create settlements in Upper California.

Gaspar de Portolá, governor of Baja California, leads his expedition north toward San Diego in 1769. Portolá begged Serra to remain behind because he feared that the padre's sore leg would cause him to slow down the expedition. Serra agreed to stay, but he set out on his own four days later.

A handful of soldiers and priests, under the overall command of Gaspar de Portolá, were to march overland from the Baja to San Diego, where they would rendezvous with two ships carrying supplies and more men. Once a mission was established there, Portolá and a couple of missionaries would continue on by land to Monterey, where a second mission would be founded and the priests could begin the work of reducing the Indians, which they estimated would take a total of 10 years. Ultimately, it was hoped, those Indians who had been converted and made loyal to Spain could be used to defend California against hostile Indians and other European colonizers. Always ambitious, Serra advised Gálvez that he hoped to ultimately establish a chain or ladder of missions, each a day's march apart from the next, along the entire length of the California coastline.

The two ships, the *San Carlos* and the *San Antonio*, departed from La Paz and Cabo San Lucas, respectively, in January 1769. The cargo manifest for the *San Antonio* has survived; among the supplies sent to found the first Spanish settlements in California were 6,500 pounds of meat and fish; several hundred bushels of corn; 5 tons of wood; a half a ton of brown sugar; dates, raisins, garlic, red pepper, cinnamon, rice, chick-peas, salt, chocolate, cheese, wine, lentils, beans, candles, and live roosters and hens.

Gálvez had changed his plans slightly, and two overland expeditions were now to be sent to meet the seagoing party at San Diego. The first, under the command of Fernando de Rivera y Moncada and consisting of 25 soldiers, Father Juan Crespí, and 44 Indian laborers, set off on March 24 from Velicatá, 350 miles south of San Diego. Portolá's party, consisting of 15 soldiers, 15 mule drivers, and 51 Baja Indians, had begun the 900-mile journey to San Diego from Loreto several weeks earlier. Conspicuous in his absence from the Portolá expedition was Serra, who had stayed behind for the official reason that he had further duties to complete before he could leave. In fact, he was virtually incapacitated by the worsening condition of his severely ulcerated left leg. Portolá, to his great sorrow, had been forced to plead with Serra to remain behind, arguing that his condition would only slow the progress of the entire party and, by delaying its passage through potentially hostile territory, possibly endanger its safety. Although Serra stubbornly insisted that God would provide him with the strength to reach not only San Diego but Monterey, he allowed the expedition to depart without him. But he would not remain behind for long.

This painting, commissioned by the city of Palma in 1790, shows Fathers Serra and Palóu at prayer. When Serra visited Palóu on his way to San Diego, Palóu feared that his friend would never survive the journey, but he underestimated Serra's toughness and determination.

CHAPTER EIGHT

"I Shall Not Turn Back"

Riding an ailing, swaybacked mule and accompanied by only two servants, Serra at last set out from Loreto to catch up with the Portolá party on March 28, 1769. ("For of all of the beasts saddled for the expedition, none were so forlorn as those they assigned me," Serra wrote.) The three expected to dine frequently at the table of the Lord, for as Serra put it, "From my mission of Loreto, I took along no more provisions for so long a journey than a loaf of bread and a piece of cheese, for I was there all year, as far as temporal matters go, as a mere guest to receive the crumbs of the royal commissary, whose liberality at my departure did not extend beyond the aforementioned articles." Obviously, despite Gálvez's revised policy, the dispute between the military and the missionaries over the control of supplies and administration continued. The military, at least on the basis of this evidence, retained the upper hand.

The determined little priest's physical condition had not greatly improved since Portolá's departure. But he had resolved, with all his considerable strength of character, that he would make it to San Diego. Ever since he had become a missionary, Serra had wished for the chance to carry the Gospel to regions whose inhabitants had never before been visited by missionaries. Portolá's expedition presented him with this opportunity, and the padre relied on all the force of his will, honed by years of self-denial, to drive himself onward, ignoring the pain in his leg and foot.

On the first night of his journey, Serra stopped at the mission of San Xavier, where his old friend and pupil Palóu was stationed. Palóu was to succeed Serra as head of the Baja missions, and Serra had been instructed by Gálvez to take the most ornate church decorations and implements from the Baja missions for use in Alta California. He had stopped off to explain this to Palóu and also to enjoy what he called the "very special and long-standing mutual affection" that existed between the two priests. Palóu was appalled when he saw the condition that his mentor and friend was in. At first he begged Serra not to continue but gave in when he concluded that, as he put it, "the fervent superior greatly exceeded me in faith and confidence in God for love of Whom he was sacrificing his life on the faith of his apostolic labors."

Their parting was sorrowful. Palóu wept as he watched two men lift the virtually crippled Serra into the saddle on his sorry mount. "Goodby, Francisco, until we meet at Monterey, where I hope we shall see each other and labor in that vineyard of the Lord," Serra called to his friend. "Goodby, Junípero, until eternity," Palóu sadly replied. But Palóu underestimated his old teacher's resilience. The two were indeed to meet again in Alta California.

It took Serra about six weeks of hard traveling to catch up with Portolá at the mission of Santa María de Los Angeles near Velicatá. For the most part, his journey took him through the central desert, an unforgiving, silent landscape more suited to maintaining the life of its plant and animal inhabitants than the small convoy of pilgrims and pack animals that was wending its weary way northward. (A mule train had been sent from Loreto after Serra's

An 18th-century artist's depiction of animals native to the California desert at the time of Serra's arduous trek to San Diego. Serra had only two Indians for company and began the trip with no more provisions than a loaf of bread and a piece of cheese.

departure; it was to be used to transport the religious items— statuary, altarpieces, vestments, bells, chalices, and so on—that Serra collected at the various Baja missions.) In the desert, the travelers encountered the giant cardon cactus; the bisnaga, or barrel cactus, which stores water in its leaves; the chirinola cactus, known as "the creeping devil"; the torete, or elephant tree; nocturnal, solitary mountain lions (called pumas by the Spanish); bands of skulking coyotes; skittish jackrabbits; herds of graceful pronghorn antelope; and an occasional bighorn sheep. Some nights, Serra stayed at a mission; other times, he camped out in the open, usually in an arroyo (the bed of a river, creek, or stream). Although arroyos were the easiest roads on which to travel, one had to be constantly alert, for a sudden thunderstorm, even at a point several miles distant, could send cascades of water roaring down upon unsuspecting wayfarers.

The journey would have been a grueling one even for a younger man in perfect health. Portolá, when Serra reached him, feared that the padre's condition would slow the progress of the entire expedition. Only one day out of Santa María, the swelling and sores on Serra's leg had reached up beyond his knee, and he was unable to wear anything but the loosest-fitting sandal on his foot. He was able to stand only to say the Mass. Portolá all but ordered him to abandon the expedition and offered to have him carried back to Santa María. Serra refused. "Your honor, please do not speak of that," he said to Portolá, "for I trust that God will give me the strength to reach San Diego, as He has given me the strength to come so far. In case He does not, I will confirm myself to His most holy will. Even though I should die on the way, *I shall not turn back.* They can bury me wherever they wish and I shall gladly be left among the pagans, if it be the will of God." Portolá relented, and Serra was carried on a stretcher by some of the Baja Indians.

After a few days of this, Serra ended his refusal to accept treatment for his condition. He had observed one of the mule drivers, Juan Antonio Coronel, preparing and applying poultices to the sore legs of the pack animals. He asked Coronel to do the same for him, and the muleteer mixed a nostrum consisting of tallow and various desert herbs, heated it, and applied the salve to Serra's wounds. That night, the priest slept without discomfort for the first time in months; soon he was able to walk and ride with considerably less pain.

Often following the trail blazed by Rivera's party, the Portolá expedition reached San Diego on July 1, 1769. Serra pronounced the harbor and bay there "truly beautiful" and "justly famous." Indeed, as the Portolá expedition had made its way north, the tireless missionary, now more than 8,000 miles away from his native

Majorca, had been overwhelmed by the increasing beauty of the land and people he encountered. The Indians were mostly "healthy and well built, affable and of happy disposition," he observed, although there were others who showed an unwelcome tendency, in the eyes of the Spanish, to pilfer goods and make menacing displays from strategic locations overlooking vulnerable arroyos.

Despite the presence of a puma that prowled outside the Spanish encampment throughout one night, the countryside was an even greater delight, "smiling with many flowers of various colors," including a small, five-petaled pink rose, the *Rosa californica*, that reminded a delighted Serra of similar species at home. "It is a good country," Serra wrote of San Diego, "very much diffcrent from the land of Old [Baja] California." Within 15 miles of San Diego, there were 20 Indian villages, surrounded by well-tended fields abounding in grain and various fruits and vegetables. Stands of willow, poplar, and sycamore trees lined the nearby riverbanks,

Monterey Bay as it appeared during the mid-19th century. As he left the desert and entered Alta California, Serra was struck by the lushness of the landscape, which reminded him of his native Majorca.

providing a home for deer, antelope, quail, and rabbits. Rivers and streams seemed to run everywhere, and the Indians also took to the sea in agile rafts to fish for sole, tuna, and sardines. The contrast to the parched landscape of the Baja could not have been greater.

Serra and his companions would not be the first newcomers to exult in the paradisiacal qualities of California, but for all the marvels of the landscape and climate, the Spanish mission at San Diego—the first permanent European settlement in what is today the state of California—at first more closely resembled hell than heaven. As planned, the *San Carlos* and *San Antonio* were anchored in San Diego Bay when the Rivera party arrived, but the condition of one of the ships was desperate. Although the *San Carlos* had departed Baja more than a month earlier than its sister ship, it did not anchor at San Diego until April 29, almost three weeks after the *San Antonio*. Its voyage had been a nightmare; by the time the vessel anchored, 24 of its 26 sailors had died from scurvy, aggravated by a lack of fresh water. (The ship's water containers had leaked soon after leaving port.) Although the death rate was not as gruesome aboard the *San Antonio*, many of its crew arrived at San Diego seriously ill from scurvy, and they continued to weaken and die after coming ashore. (Scurvy is caused by a lack of vitamin C in the diet; until the 19th century, sailors on long voyages were especially prone to the affliction because of their lack of access to fresh food.) When the Rivera and then the Portolá parties arrived, those members of the seagoing expedition who possessed sufficient strength were engaged in the grim work of burying the dead. Serra's first task at San Diego was therefore tending to the sick.

The overland parties had fared considerably better, if one did not consider the welfare of the Indians who accompanied them. All the Spanish members of the Rivera and Portolá expeditions made it to San Diego safely, but only 12 of the 44 Indians who accompanied Rivera, and only 13 of the 51 who accompanied Portolá, got through the journey. It is uncertain what proportion of the missing Indians died and what proportion deserted along the way, but it is

Serra dedicated the mission of San Diego, the first permanent European settlement in what is now the state of California, on July 16, 1769. Before he could begin the work of conversion, however, he had to bury those members of the Portolá expedition who had contracted scurvy while at sea.

certain that the Indians were severely mistreated. Although they performed all of the most strenuous physical labor for the expedition—most were employed as human pack animals—they were largely expected to fend for themselves as far as food was concerned. Occasionally, the Spaniards were moved to give them a little *atole*, an unappetizing cornmeal mush that was described by Father Crespí, who accompanied and chronicled the Rivera expedition, as "more water than gruel."

The leather-jacketed Spanish soldiers survived the overland trek in good shape, however, and within two weeks of his arrival at San Diego, Portolá was ready to push on to Monterey, chosen by Gálvez as the most crucial site at which to establish the Spanish presence in California. Serra remained behind; on July 16, in a mass punctuated by rifle volleys at appropriate points, he formally dedicated the mission of San Diego. A number of small log huts, roofed with tule (a variety of bulrush), were hastily erected; most served as dwellings, although one functioned as a chapel and another as a hospital.

Serra wasted no time in beginning the work of conversion, but his zeal was not immediately rewarded. Although the local Indians often wandered in to have a look around, they remained wary and refused to accept even the smallest morsel of food. No doubt, they considered the large number of graves and sick and dying men a warning to the prudent. In mid-August, after observing that the mission's garrison had been reduced to only four soldiers, the Indians attacked. Serra described in a letter to Father Juan Andrés the death of his servant, whose neck was pierced by an arrow: "He entered into my little hut with so much blood streaming from his temples and mouth that shortly after I gave him absolution. . . . He passed away at my feet, bathed in his blood. . . . All during this time, the exchange of shots from the firearms and arrows continued. . . . I continued to stay with the departed one, thinking over the imminent probability of following him myself, yet I kept begging God to give victory to our Holy Catholic faith without the loss of a single soul."

This early-19th-century drawing shows a group of mission Indians betting on a game played with sticks. Though they attacked the mission only once, the San Diego Indians remained wary of the Spaniards. Serra labored for an entire year before he made his first conversion.

Despite their advantage in numbers, the Indians were driven off by the superior Spanish firepower. Three of the Indians had been killed; the soldiers kept this news from Serra, who would have been greatly upset to know that they had died without being baptized. After their unsuccessful attack, the Indians became somewhat more friendly, but the San Diego Indians always remained among the most resistant of the California peoples to Spanish reduction, and Serra was not to succeed in making his first conversion there for more than a year. Until Portolá returned, the Spaniards lived in constant fear of another attack, and many preferred the relative safety of the two ships in the harbor to the precarious existence on land. Even Serra admitted, in a letter to Palóu, the difficulty of the situation: "We have tortillas on the table and vegetables in the garden. What more could we wish? But to be without any news from anywhere; . . . not knowing if we will be able to hold what we have so far gained—that is what distresses us."

Portolá's party of 74 returned to San Diego on January 24, 1770. Every member of the expedition had survived, although they carried with them the "frightful smell of mules," for supplies had grown short and they had been forced to slaughter their pack animals for food. The party had covered 900 miles, discovering the sites of the future cities of Los Angeles and San Francisco, but had failed to locate Monterey. "You come from Rome without seeing the Pope," cried a disappointed Serra, who had begun to fear for the success of the mission effort in California. Within a few weeks, he had even greater cause for alarm, for the *San Antonio*, which had been sent back to the Baja for supplies, had failed to return, and Portolá announced that San Diego would have to be abandoned. On March 19, sentries spotted the sails of the *San Antonio* on the horizon. An overjoyed Serra celebrated the ship's arrival with a high mass.

With San Diego resupplied and provided with a strengthened garrison, Portolá resolved to search for Monterey once more. He led an expedition overland, while the *San Antonio*, with Serra aboard, sailed north along the coast. Once again Portolá made the northward march without the loss of a single man, and he arrived at Monterey on May 24. (He had, in fact, been there on his first expedition and had even planted a cross there, but he had not recognized it as being Monterey.) The *San Antonio* arrived a week later, with all of its party in relatively good health, although some were showing the first signs of scurvy. When all were united, Serra presided over a ceremony that he described exultantly in a letter to Palóu:

> My happiness was complete when on the Holy Feast of the
> Pentecost, June 3, all the sea and land officers, together
> with all their men, came in a body to the little valley and oak
> tree where the Fathers of Viscaíno's expedition celebrated
> Mass [in 1603]. After preparing the altar, and hanging the
> bells from the branches of the tree, we sang the hymn *Veni,
> Creator* and blessed the holy water. We then raised aloft and
> blessed a great cross, likewise the royal standards. After that
> I celebrated the first Mass that is known to have been sung
> there since the Viscaíno expedition. . . . The function came
> to a conclusion with the singing of the *Te Deum*. After that,
> the officers performed the official act of taking possession
> of the country in the name of the King our Lord, may God
> preserve him. . . . Later on we all ate together at a shady
> spot on the beach, and the whole feast was accompanied by
> the firing of the guns both on land and on the boat.

Over the next several weeks, the Spanish began constructing a permanent mission and presidio at a site selected by Serra, several miles south of Monterey, near present-day Carmel. There, on December 26, 1770, Serra performed his first baptism in California.

News that missions had been established at San Diego and Monterey was greeted with joy in Mexico City, where the church bells tolled in celebration for an entire day. For the next 13 years, Serra, his fellow priests, and Spanish soldiers, combining brutal force with gentle persuasion, were to carry on the work of reducing

On June 3, 1770, Father Serra (standing at altar) dedicated the San Carlos mission at Monterey with a mass under the Vizcaíno oak. At this ceremony, Spain formally claimed Alta California and began to put its mark on the territory that would later become part of the United States.

California's Indians, whose numbers and variety were unmatched anywhere else in the lands that eventually became the United States of America. In that period Serra, most of the time in person, presided over the establishment of nine missions—in addition to San Diego and San Carlos de Carmel (Monterey), he founded San Antonio de Padua (July 1771), San Gabriel (September 1771), San Luis Obispo (September 1772), San Francisco (October 1776), San Juan Capistrano (November 1776), Santa Clara (January 1777), and San Buenaventura (March 1782).

Despite his advancing age and declining health, Serra traveled frequently between the missions, exhorting his colleagues to increase their efforts to convert the Indians. Under his direction permanent churches were built, fields were planted, settlements begun. He was tireless in defending the missions and his missionaries from interference from the military commanders, who were inclined to control the Indians by force and were usually reluctant to provide enough soldiers to establish and protect new missions. In 1773, with the support of the Spanish viceroy, Chevalier Antonio María Bucareli y Ursúa, Serra drew up a legal brief asserting the power of the missions and placing the care of the Indians exclusively in the hands of the priests. Due to Serra's rapport with Bucareli, military commanders who opposed Serra's views found themselves in trouble with the colonial government in Mexico City. Fernando de Rivera, a commander whom the priests excommunicated for arresting an Indian under their protection, complained about Serra in terms the padre would have considered highly complimentary: "I have never seen a priest more zealous for founding missions than this Father President. He thinks of nothing but founding missions, no matter how or at what expense they are established."

Serra died of an unrecorded illness—possibly lung cancer—on August 28, 1784, at the mission of San Carlos, in the company of his faithful friend Palóu. Shortly before he expired on his crude wooden bed, clutching his crucifix to his chest as always, he said to Palóu: "I promise, if the Lord in His infinite mercy grants me eternal happiness, which I do not deserve because of my sins and faults, that I shall pray for all [those at the missions] and for the conversion of so many whom I leave unconverted." At the time of his death, thousands of baptisms and confirmations had been performed at Serra's missions, although the Indian funerals presided over by the dedicated missionaries always outnumbered the births. California's Indian population, an estimated 250,000 at the time the Spanish arrived, plummeted at about the same rate as in Spain's other dominions, for roughly the same reasons.

Although Serra died in the certainty that California was securely under Spanish control, in a few short years Spain's New World empire began to break asunder. In 1848, California became part of the United States, whose inhabitants—a mixture of people from

Junípero Serra (kneeling, right center) receives Holy Communion from Father Francisco Palóu, shortly before Serra's death at the San Carlos mission. Palóu comforted his old friend during his final hours and administered the last rites to him.

many nations—would be no less ruthless in their treatment of the Indians than the Spanish had been. Nevertheless, Serra's original missions still stand, thanks in large part to restoration work performed during the late 19th century; their simple but dramatic architecture has been duplicated in public and private buildings throughout California and the Southwest. Many place names in the state of California, such as Santa Clara, San Gabriel, and San Luis Obispo, commemorate Serra's activities, and the settlements he established at San Diego and San Francisco have grown into important cities. His role in the growth of California and the United States has been commemorated by a number of statues, including one in the Statuary Hall of the Capitol in Washington, D.C. In 1963, the U.S. Congress ordered the creation of a medal to commemorate the 250th anniversary of Serra's birth. It was the first time such a national honor had been accorded to a Catholic priest.

In 1934, Junípero Serra was put forward as a candidate for canonization as a saint of the Catholic church, a process that takes many years and requires rigorous examination of the candidate's life and activities. Finally, in 1986, the church announced its intention to beatify Father Serra, beatification being the final step before sainthood. This news drew immediate protests from American Indian groups, who objected that the Spanish and their missionaries had tried to eradicate the native inhabitants and their culture; they particularly pointed to accounts of Indians being rounded up and whipped as a means of forcing them to attend church. The controversy intensified in 1987, when Pope John Paul II visited the mission of San Carlos during his trip to the United States and prayed at Father Serra's grave. Proceeding to Phoenix, Arizona, he met with representatives of Indian groups and defended Serra's legacy. Admitting that excesses had been committed during Serra's administration of the missions, the pope insisted that Serra himself had never been guilty of maltreating the Indians and had often protected them from the soldiers. He characterized Serra as a great man.

Indian critics were not satisfied with the pope's assurances and demanded that more research be done before beatification. When the church declined to honor this request, a spokeswoman for the American Indian Historical Society complained, "The pope doesn't care about what's been done to us." Despite all protests, the ceremony of beatification—conducted by the pope and attended by a delegation of 500 Californians—took place on September 25, 1988, on the steps of St. Peter's Basilica in Rome, Italy. Junípero Serra thereby became the subject of public prayer and veneration for Roman Catholics. Although the controversy over his prospective sainthood is likely to continue, Junípero Serra's role in the settlement of North America remains secure.

Chronology

Nov. 24, 1713	Born Miguel José Serra on the island of Majorca
1730	Begins his novitiate at the Franciscan Convent of Jesus
1731	Takes his vows as a Franciscan monk; takes the name Junípero
1734	Ordained as a subdeacon
1736	Ordained as a deacon
1737	Becomes a full priest; takes a teaching position at the Convent of San Francisco in Majorca
1742	Receives his doctorate in theology from the University of Ramon Llull
April–Dec. 1749	With Francisco Palóu, departs for the territories of New Spain—Texas and Mexico—to begin his missionary work
1750–58	Reaches the Apostolic College of San Fernando in Mexico City on foot from Veracruz; volunteers to run the missions of the Sierra Gorda; substitutes Catholic rituals

	and places of worship for those used byIndians in order to convert them to Christianity; oversees the construction of a church in Jalpan
1759–67	Summoned to Mexico City by the Apostolic College of San Fernando, where he serves for nine years as choirmaster and supervisor of novices
1767	Spanish officials in Mexico, acting under the orders of King Charles III, expel the Jesuits from Spain and all Spanish territories in the Americas
1768	Serra is sent to Baja California to occupy a mission formerly run by the Jesuits; plans to establish a mission in San Diego in what is now the state of California
1769–70	Reaches San Diego in July; from San Diego goes on to Monterey; performs his first baptism in California
1770–82	Presides over the establishment of nine missions along the California coast, including San Luis Obispo, San Francisco, and San Juan Capistrano; travels frequently between the missions despite failing health
Aug. 28, 1784	Dies, possibly of lung cancer, at the mission of San Carlos
Sept. 25, 1988	Beatified—the last step before canonization in the Catholic church—by Pope John Paul II

Further Reading

Ainsworth, Katherine, and Edward C. Ainsworth. *In the Shade of the Juniper Tree*. Garden City, NY: Doubleday, 1970.

Bowden, Dina Moore. *Junípero Serra in His Native Isle*. Palma de Majorca, Spain: Moore, 1976.

Clough, Charles W. *Madera: The Rich, Colorful, and Exciting Historical Heritage of That Area Now Known as Madera County, California*. Fresno, CA: Panorama West, 1983.

Culleton, James H. *Indians and Pioneers of Old Monterey*. Fresno, CA: Panorama West, 1950.

Duque, Sarah. *Sally and Father Serra*. Valencia, CA: Tabor, 1987.

Engstrand, Iris H. *Serra's San Diego: Father Junípero Serra and California's Beginning*. San Diego: San Diego Historical Society, 1982.

Habig, Marion A. *Junípero Serra*. Chicago: Franciscan Herald Press, 1987.

Lyngheim, Linda, et al. *Father Junípero Serra, the Traveling Missionary.* Van Nuys, CA: Langtry, 1986.

Moholy, Noel Francis, and Don DeNevi. *Junípero Serra: The Illustrated Story of the Franciscan Founder of California's Missions.* New York: HarperCollins, 1985.

Morgado, Martin J. *Junípero Serra's Legacy.* Pacific Grove, CA: Mt. Carmel, 1987.

Morrill, Sibley S. *The Texas Cannibals, or, Why Father Serra Came to California.* Oakland: Holmes, 1964.

Paz, Octavio. *Sor Juana: Or, the Traps of Faith.* Cambridge: Harvard University Press, 1988.

Scott, Bernice. *Junípero Serra: Pioneer of the Cross.* Fresno, CA: Panorama West, 1985.

Tibesar, Antonine, ed. *Writings of Junípero Serra.* Bethesda, MD: Academy of American Franciscan History, 1966.

Index

SEAN DOLAN holds a degree in history and literature from the State University of New York. He is the author of several books on the subject of world exploration, including biographies of the explorers Christopher Columbus and Matthew Henson.

RODOLFO CARDONA is professor of Spanish and comparative literature at Boston University. A renowned scholar, he has written many works of criticism, including *Ramón, a Study of Gómez de la Serna and His Works* and *Visión del esperpento: Teoría y práctica del esperpento en Valle-Inclán*. Born in San José, Costa Rica, he earned his B.A. and M.A. from Louisiana State University and received a Ph.D. from the University of Washington. He has taught at Case Western Reserve University, the University of Pittsburgh, the University of Texas at Austin, the University of New Mexico, and Harvard University.

JAMES COCKCROFT is currently a visiting professor of Latin American and Caribbean studies at the State University of New York at Albany. A three-time Fulbright scholar, he earned a Ph.D. from Stanford University and has taught at the University of Massachusetts, the University of Vermont, and the University of Connecticut. He is the author or coauthor of numerous books on Latin American subjects, including *Neighbors in Turmoil: Latin America*, *The Hispanic Experience in the United States: Contemporary Issues and Perspectives*, and *Outlaws in the Promised Land: Mexican Immigrant Workers and America's Future*.

PICTURE CREDITS